SWAMI VIVEKANANDA

SWAMI VIVEKANANDA

By

N.L. GUPTA

ANMOL PUBLICATIONS PVT. LTD.
NEW DELHI - 110 002 (INDIA)

ANMOL PUBLICATIONS PVT. LTD.
4374/4B, Ansari Road, Daryaganj
New Delhi - 110 002
Ph.: 23261597, 23278000
Visit us: www.anmolpublications.com

Swami Vivekananda

First Edition, 2003

ISBN 81-261-1538-6

PRINTED IN INDIA

Published by J.L. Kumar for Anmol Publications Pvt. Ltd., New Delhi - 110 002 and Printed at Tarun Offset Printers, (Delhi)

Contents

Preface

Swami Vivekananda was not only a revivalist like Rammohun Roy, Tilak and others; but an awakened spirit of India, a synthesis of orientalism and modernity. In him we find fusion of nationalism, patriotism and spiritualism. The harmony of all religions, which Ramakrishna Paramhansa accomplished in his life's endeavour, was the key-note of his life, which was followed by him in all the spheres of his multifarious activities. He was a good social scientist also. Thus he could diagnose the main causes of India's ruin such as caste-system, monopoly of the brahmins in the field of knowledge and education. Therefore, he stressed on the spreading of education among the downtroddens and the backward classes, who were deprived of this privilege for centuries due to rigid caste-system and other social evils, Dr. V.K.R.V. Rao calls it a 'Vedantic Socialism'. In fact, socialism cannot work well or be lasting without spiritualism.

Similarly he showed his great concern for the education of women-folk. To him 'to know' and 'to do' are very synonymous. He not only pleaded for women education through his speeches and writings; but also got himself involved in this noble cause. He established Ramkrishna Mission, which is running hundreds of schools and colleges in the country and abroad. Streamlining the aims of Ramkrishna Mission once (May 1897) he said:

> "The aim of the Association is to preach those truths, which Shri Ramkrishna was, for the good of humanity, given out and demonstrated by practical application in his own life, and to help those truth's being made practical in the lives of others for their temporal, mental and spiritual advancement."

Hence the spirit of propaganda was established in the doctrine whose essence is "the establishment of fellowship among the followers of different religions, knowing them all to be so many forms only of one undying Eternal Religion.

In this volume an attempt has been made to present the critique of educational ideas of Swami Vivekananda. In the appendix some extracts from his speeches and writing have been reproduced. Besides three appendices there are ten chapters in this book which cover almost all the aspects of educational thought of Swami Vivekananda. His educational thought has very great significance today because modern education has lost much of its connection with human values whereas value-oriented education is the need of the hour as felt by the educationist. The present system of education is nothing but a machine for turning out some diploma or degree holders, who have no faith in themselves. Vivekananda denounced this system and emphasised the need for a complete re-orientation of human values to fight against hedonism and commercial fetishes. He suggested that education should not be for stuffing some information or facts into the brain, it should aim at reforming the human mind and unfolding of the personality. He criticized such education which is not related to the real life-situations and nature of the people or community the students live in. He calls such education fertile which enable the student to know the name of private secretary of the queen Elizabeth I; but does not inspire him to know the names of his forefathers.

This is the sixth book in the series styled as " *Encyclopaedia of Modern Educational Thinkers of India*". The author will take his effort fruitful if it is also liked by the esteemed readers, like its other counterparts. The author is grateful to all those authors is grateful to all those authors and scholar's whose works have been helpful in writing this volume. Last but not the least, author's thanks are due to Shri J.L. Kumar of Anmol Publications Pvt. Ltd., who inspired the author to take-up this big project.

—**Dr. N.L. Gupta**

1

Swami Vivekananda: The Man and His Mission

"One can understand India better by studying Swami Vivekananda; His teachings are linked up with spiritual and physical experiences with their stress on cultivation of purity and strength. While conducting a crusade for the betterment of the fallen, the suppressed and the poor, Vivekananda saw that 'Renunciation' and 'Service' must be twin ideas of India. He wanted reformation of Indian society, root and branch."

—*Rabindranath Tagore*

"Triumph of Vivekananda in the Western world is the indicative of the phenomena that India is awakened not only to escape from mortality but to win over the world at spiritual plane."

—*Shri Aurobindo*

"It is pious duty of the Hindu community that till it is alive it should cherish the memory of Vivekananda with the same reverence as it is remembering Vyas and Valmiki."

—*Ramadhari Singh 'Dinkar'*

"Much has happened which perhaps makes some forget those who came before and who prepared India and shaped India in those early and difficult days. If you read Swami Vivekananda's writings and speeches, the curious thing you will find is that they are not old. It was told 56 years ago, and they are fresh today because, what he wrote and spoke about dealt certain fundamental matters and aspects of our problems or the world problems. Therefore, they do not become old. They are fresh even though you read them now."

—Jawaharlal Nehru, from the speech delivered in 1949 at Calcutta.

"He coined the world which is very commonly used in our Indian English—'don't touchism'. His heart overflowed with love and sympathy for the masses, whom he wanted to serve with religious zeal—serve as a believer in the Vedanta which sees God in all life. He coined a new word for our Indian Languages—'Daridra-Narayan or a God in the poor and lowly'. This word has been accepted by the whole of India, and in a way in a sense of responsibility for the average man. He has to look upon poor and the humble, the sufferings ones of society; as if they were deities incarnate or fragments of God."

—Suniti Kumar Chatterji, Swami Vivekananda Centenary Memorial Volume, p. 230.

From his early years Narendranath Dutt, later known as Swami Vivekananda, proved a voracious reader with a prodigious memory. He came under the influence of Ramakrishna Paramhansa and after his master's death organised the Ramakrishna Mission. He was pained to see the decadent state of Hindu society. He anguished call to the nation was: 'O India! Forget not that the lower classes, the ignorant, the poor, the illiterate, the cobbler, the sweeper are thy flesh and blood'. He saw the divine in the form of the poor whom he called Daridra Narayan.

It was 11 September 1893, the opening day of the Parliament of Religions held in Chicago. Swamiji sat rapt in silent meditation. In the late afternoon he rose to speak. He bowed down to Devi Saraswati and addressed his audience as, 'Sisters and Brothers of America'. And before he could utter another word, the whole Parliament was taken by a great storm of enthusiasm. Hundreds upon hundreds rose to their feet and sent up deafening notes of applause. For full 2 minutes he attempted to speak but the wild enthusiasm of the audience provented him. When silence was restored he began this short address.

At the time to Parliament of Religions, Vivekananda was only thirty years old. He was born in Calcutta on 12th January, 1863. His name was Narendranath Dutta. He assumed the name of Vivekananda only just before embarking for U.S.A., at the suggestion of the Maharaja of Khetri, who, with the Maharaja of Mysore, paid expenses of his journey. He possessed grand and good looking personality. He was also a fine singer and could play several musical instruments. His teachers predicted that he was destined to become a great man.

At that time the activities of Brahmo Samaj was making good headway. To meet the challenge of missionary Christianity, a movement had been launched to modernise Hinduism to do away with ancient ritual and preistcraft, to emancipate women, and to abolish child marriage. Narendra joined it, but soon found its aims superficial; they did not satisfy his own spiritual need. He read Hume, Herbert Spencer, and John Stuart Mill, and began to call himself an agnostic. His parents urged him to marry, but he refused, feeling that he must remain chaste and unattached so as to be ready to devote himself body and soul to a great cause of humanity. According to him "to serve humanity is to serve God."

It so happened that Naren's relative was a devotee of Ramakrishna, and Professor Hasties, one of Naren's teachers spoke very high of Ramakrishna, which excited his curiosity. In November 1881, he was invited to sing at a house, where Ramakrishna was a guest. They had a brief conversation and

Ramakrishna invited the young men to come and visit him at Dakshineshwar Temple, on the bank of the Ganges, at the distance of a few miles from Calcutta, where he lived. Naren did so and thereafter such meetings became frequent and ultimately he became his chief disciple. At the time of death Ramakrishna made him heir apparent and chief monk of Dakshineswar.

Even after his grand success in America and other European countries when he returned to India he never forgot who he was: the disciple of Ramakrishna and the equal brother of his fellow monks. On 1st May 1897 he called a meeting of the monastic and householder disciples of Ramakrishna in order to establish their work on an organised basis. What Vivekananda prosposed was an integration of educational, philanthropic, and religious activities; and it was thus that the Ramakrishna Mission and the Ramakrishna Math, or monastery came into existence. The mission went to work immediately, taking part in famine and plague relief and founding its first hospitals and schools. Brahmananda was elected as its president, and to him Vivekananda handed over all the money he had collected in America and Europe.

Regarding the impact of Vedanta on the modern Indian thought the following observations of Swami Vivekananda are noteworthy:

- Vedanta can be carried into our everyday life, the city life, the country life and the home life of every nation. (II: 300)
- These conceptions of Vedanta must come out, must remain not only in the forest, not only in the cave, but they must come out to work at the Bar and the Bench in the pulpit and in the cottage of the poor man. (III: 245)
- The philosophy, which cannot solve the problems of human life, which cannot shed away the prejudices of mankind such religion and philosophy are useless and meaningless in the present-day society. (II: 291)

Vivekananda rightly called such philosophy merely "intellectual gymnastics. It reveals his concern about mankind and he was all out to benefit a man by reviving the concept of religion and philosophy. This is the most striking feature of his philosophy that he brought the philosophy of Vedanta from the permit to house, from scholar to a lay man, from sophistication to simplicity from theory to practice. Above all the harnessed all his resources, material and spiritual, inner and outer, for the common good of the common man. Describing the main components of his simple religion he says:

"Each soul is potentially divine.

The goal is to manifest this divinity.

Within by controlling nature, external and internal.

Do this either by work or worship or psychic control

Or philosophy by one or more or all of these and be free.

This is the whole of religion. Doctrines or dogmas or rituals

Or books or temples or forms are but secondary details."[1]

In the above quotation we find the most of the elements of the revived Hinduism for which all the revivalists struggled for decades. Eventually it can be said that with Swami Vivekananda the Hindu revivalist movement attained adolescence and self-consciousness. The Brahmo Samaj could not send down deep roots in the Hindu soil. The Arya Samaj was the first articulate and vigorous expression of Hindu revivalism in India; yet it could not provide Hindu religion with ideological coherence and spiritual grandeur. Hinduism gained in militancy but needed more vigour and rigour. It was the major achievement of Swami Vivekananda to have given it sobriety, prestige and the firmness of ideological foundation.

Emancipation of Women

Though the Vedanta declares that both men and women have the same self in them is much difference in India between them than anywhere in the world. In the Vedic and Upanishadic age, women enjoyed almost every privilege as men but later the priests had deprived them of their rights. A country's greatness is usually judged by the way in which it shows respect towards her women. In America men look upon their women in this light and treat them well.

The principal reason why India has degenerated is that there is no respect for women. The women of India have long been trained in helplessness and servile dependence on others. Education along can solve their many and varied problems. To Vivekananda, "Women must be put in their own way and Indian women are as capable of doing it as any in the world."

India requires great and fearless women to continue the traditions of Ahalya Bai and Mira Bai women fit to be mothers of heroes bound by the principles of chastity and purity. Education of women should be spread with religion as its centre. It may go a long way in the formation of character and observance of celebacy.

The ideal of a perfect women is to be found in Sita, in the great epic Ramayana, and every Indian women should try to attain that greatness and strength. In the Vedic or Upanishadic ages also there were similar examples like Maitreyi and Gargi who had taken the place of rishis through their wonderful eruditions in philosophy. The first thing, that is required, is to intensify this ideal of womahood in the Indian women so that they may feel the necessity of coming up along with men. Along with that they should be taught the sciences and other things which would be of real use to them.

Considering the needs of his age, Vivekananda feels it imperative to train some women in the ideals of renunciation in order that they may work as Brahmacharinis for women's welfare and progress. In his opinion society in every country shapes its destiny. "So we need not trouble our heads about such reforms as the abolition of early marriage or the remarriage of widows". The main task of India is to impact education to both men and women alike. As an outcome of that education, they will be able to decide what is good for them. In the education of women can be included subject like Religion, Arts, science, Home-management, Cooking, Sewing and Hygiene. For this trained brahmacharinis should go to be villages and towns, open centres, and do hard work. Along with other thing, Japa, worship and meditation shall form an indispensable part of teaching.

Vivekananda hopes that the women who get themselves trained in these centres will make further progress in the virtues that distinguish them from the rest. The children of such mothers will prove themselves to be worthy citizens of India. "It is only in the hands of educated and pious mother that great men are born." The ideal women in India is mother, the mother first and the mother last. From this mother-hood comes tremendous responsibility on women. The mother is the ideal of love. She rules the family, she possesses the family, "To the ordinary man in India, the whole force of womanhood is concentrated in motherhood."

No women should any longer remain content in an inferior position. In most of the Western countries women have gained considerable importance in their race for equality with men. But blind imitation of the West cannot be equated with the social progress of India. In the West the spiritual aims of human life are not uppermost as it is India. It is the spiritual ideal of Sita that Indian women have been following through the ages. Faith in god self abnegation and service have marked their character, and chastity has been the guiding motive of their life.

Thoughts

- External worship of images has, however, been described in all our shastra at the lowest of all the low forms of worship. But that does not mean that it is a wrong thing to do.[2]
- Where should you go to seek for God? Are not all the poor, miserable, the weak, Gods? Why not worship them first? Why go to dig a well on the shores of the Ganga? Let these people be your God-think of them incessantly- the Lord will show you the way.

- My ideal indeed can be put into a few words and that is: to preach unto mankind their divinity, and how to make it manifest in every movement of life.
- The religion, the idea which is raising brute unto man, and man unto god.
- So long as the millions die in hunger and ignorance. I hold every man a traitor who, having been educated at their expense, pays not the least heed to them.
- The least you read the better. Read the Geeta and other good works on the Vedanta. That is all you need. The present system of education is all wrong. The mind is crammed with facts before it knows how to think. Control of the mind should be taught first. If I had my education to get over again and had any voice in the matter, I would to master my mind first, and then greater facts if I wanted them.
- The secret of religion lies not in theories but in practices. To be good and to do good—that is whole religion. Not he that crieth 'Lord', 'Lord', but he that doeth the will of the Father.[3]
- Be moral. Be brave. Be a heart-whole man. Strictly moral, brave unto desperation. Don't bother your head with religious theories. Cowards only sin, brave men never, no not even in mind.[4]
- Doing good to other is virtue (Dharma), injuring others is sin. Strength and manliness are virtue; weakness and cowardice is sin. Loving others is virtue, hating others is sin. Faith in God and in one's self is virtue; doubt is sin. Knowledge of oneness is virtue; seeing diversity is sin."[5]
- He who wants to serve the father must serve the children first. He who wants to serve Shiva must serve his children must serve all creatures in this world first. It is said in the Shastras that those who serve the servants of God are his greatest servants. So you will

bear this in mind. Let me tell you again that you must be pure and help anyone, who comes to you, as much as lies in your power. And this is good karma. By the power of this, the heart becomes pure (chitta-shuddhi) and then Shiva who is residing in every one will become manifest… And if a man is selfish, even thought he has visited all the temples, seen all the places of pilgrimage and painted himself like a leopard, he is further off from Shiva.[6]

- For our mother lands, a junction of the two great systems Hinduism and Islam Vedanta brain and Islamic body is the only hope.[7]
- Men can never be united unless there is a bond of common interest, you can never unite people merely by getting up meetings, societies and lecture, if their interest be not one and the same.
- The more advanced a society or nation is in spirituality, the more is that society or nation civilised, No nation can be said to have become civilised only because it has succeeded in increasing the comforts of material life by bringing into use of machinery and things of that sort.[8]
- I shall call you religious from the you began to see God in men and women and then you will understand what is meant by turning the left cheek to the man who strikes you on right. When you seen as good everything, even the tiger, will be welcome.[9]
- The ideal of womanhood is mother. In the west it is the wife. Where is she in your country who would give ten times or even more, her life for her child? Where is she compared to the one who would go to the divorce court the moment you treat her a little badly, where is she? Where is she? I don't find her country ! Oh! America, where is she?[10]
- You can reach god by playing football than through the study of Geeta".

- For the next years...let all other vain Gods disappear for time from our minds. This is only God that is awake, our own race everywhere. His hands, everywhere his feet, everywhere his ears, he covers everythings . All other Gods are sleeping. What vain Gods shall we go after and yet cannot worship the God that we see all round us, the Virat?... of those all around us... These are all our gods men and animals, and the first god we have to worship are our own countrymen...[12]

Address at Chango on 11th Sep. 1893

Sisters and Brothers of America,

It fills my heart with joy unspeakable to rise in response to the warm and cordial welcome which you have given us. I thank you in the name of the most ancient order of monks in the world; I think you in the name of the mother of religions; and I thank you in the name of millions and millions of Hindu people of all classes and sects.

My thanks, also to some of the speakers on this platform who, referring to the delegates from the orient, have told you that these men from far off nations may well claim the honour of bearing to different lands the ideas of toleration. I am proud to belong to a religion which has taught the world both tolerance and universal toleration, but we accept all religions as true. I am proud to belong to a nation as true. I am proud to belong to a nation which has sheltered the persecuted and the refugees of all religions and all nations of the earth. I am proud to tell you that we have gathered in our bosom the purest remanant of the Israelites, who came to Southern India and took refuge with us in the very year in which their holy temple was shattered to pieces by Roman tyranny. I am proud to belong to the religion which has sheltered and is still fostering the remnant of the grand Zoroastrian nation. I will quote to you, brethren, a few lines from a hymn which I remember to have repeated from my earliest boyhood which is every day repeated by millions of human beings; "As the different streams having their sources in different place all mingle their water in the sea, so, O Lord, the different paths which men take through different tendencies, various though they appear, crooked or straight, all lead to Thee."

The present convention, which is one of the most august assemblies ever held, is in itself a vindication, a declaration to the world of the wonderful doctrine preached in the Gita. "Whosoever comes to Me, through whatsoever form, I reach him; all men are struggling through paths which in the end lead to me." Sectarianism, bigotry, and its horrible descendant, fanaticism, have long possessed this beautiful earth. They have filled the earth with violence, drenched it often and often and often with human blood, destroyed civilisation and sent whole nations to despair. Had it not been for these horrible demons, human society would be for more advanced than it is now. But their time is come; and I fervently hope that the bell that tolled this morning in honour of this convention may be the death knell of all fanaticism, of all fanaticism, of all persecutions with the sword or with the pen, and of all uncharitable feelings between persons wending their way to the same goal.

REFERENCES

1. John Yale, *What Religion Is*? p. 1.
2. *Complete Works of Swami Vivekananda*, Vol II. p. 74.
3. *Ibid*, Vol. VI, p. 245.
4. *Ibid*, Vol. V, p. 3.
5. *Ibid*, Vol. V, p. 419.
6. *Ibid*, Vol. III, p. 141.
7. V.K.R.V. Rao, *Swami Vivekananda*, p. 240.
8. *Ibid*, p. 195.
9. *Complete Works*, Vol. II, p. 324.
10. Complete works of Swami Vivekananda—Vol.II, p. 300.
12. *Ibid*, Vol. III, p. 245.
13. *Ibid*, Vol.II, p. 291.

2
Vivekananda and Universal Religion

Poets are the legislators of the world, said Shelley. We may that saints are the architects of the world. The world is being wielded by politicians no doubt, but it is being moulded by the teaching of the saints. The holy men sustain this world by their teachings manifested through their speech or conduct. Every human being, high or low, is influenced in some measure by some holy man or the other. Even kings require the blessings of saints. That is why Gandhiji says that politics must be spiritualised and Plato insists that philosophers must be kings and kings should be philosophers. In the world of Mathew Arnold a king must, like the scholar gypsy, drink the milk of Paradise. It is the function of the saints to supply the milk of paradise to the people who are lost in the forest of the madding crow, be he a prince or a pauper.

Saints are of three categories. Meditative, Devotee or Missionary. Meditative saints are those who ponder in isolation over the infinite and seek their own personal salvation—society is away from their mind and body. Suka Muni was one of them. There are a number of nameless similar philosopher-saints. Devotee saints are in love with God and they bother neither about their own salvation nor about that of the society. They are so much in tune with the personal God, that their love to god makes them blind to the society. Meerabai was such a type.

But there is a third variety of the tribe of the holy men who preach religion and strive for the salvation of the society. They have a set mission in life. They have not only devotion but dedication too. Kipling gloated over the white mans burden to redeem the ignorant blossoms from the dust of darkness. They are saints imbued with a social consciousness. Swami Vivekananda was a missionary-saint.

Swamiji was a great Hindu, a greater Vedantist and one of the greatest of the missionary saints of India. His twin faiths in life were *reason* and *freedom*.

He believed in the unity of religions and hence advocated the ideal of a universal religion. His outlook was throughout rational, like the great Sankaracarya. In his talk, "Reason and Religion," he has stated that religion is to justify itself by the discoveries of reason, through which every other science justifies itself. He remarks that the same method of investigation which we apply to science and knowledge outside should be applied to the science of religion. According to Swamiji the religion of the Vedanta stands this test of reason.[1]

Swamiji believed not only in reason but also in the freedom of thought, expression and action. He also championed the freedom of faith regularly for prayers, meditations and discussions. Here, he founded the Baranagore Math and organised a *Sangha* or brotherhood consisting mainly of young brother-disciples, who would meet there to perform *Sadhana* and *Bhajan* regularly.

In order to get a first-hand knowledge of the social, economic and religious conditions as also the past glory and heritage of India, he wanted to see all places of historical interest, all important religious and holy places, temples, monasteries and tombs. Accordingly, he set out on a journey to different parts of India. It was from this time, Narendra Nath, clad in a traveller's dress, came to be known as Swami Vivekananda.

In the course of his journey throughout India he came in contact with the various types of men—high and low, Rajas and Maharajas, rich and poor, peasants and labourers and men of different castes, colours and creeds. The various religious places and the innumerable temples, monasteries and tombs which he visited provided him with a glimpse of India's past glory and heritage in art and culture. This journey also provided him with a picture of the miserable condition of the people in every sphere of their lives. Abject poverty, illiteracy, complete absence of political consciousness, crude and mistaken ideas about religion which he noticed left an indelible impression on his mind.

This journey of instruction decided his future course of action. He realised that India could offer her spiritual wealth to Western countries which had misconceptions about India's religion, culture and civilisation, and import from them scientific knowledge and instruments for economic regeneration of the country. Naturally, therefore, he was thinking of visiting countries of the West. It was during his journey in southern part of India, that he heard that a World Religious Congress would be held at Chicago in America soon. He thought of attending the conference as representative of Hindu religion and culture. Providence fulfilled his desire. He was invited to the Congress to represent the Hindu religion. In his memorable speech at the conference, he explained the essential features of Hinduism—its tolerant, catholic and universal character as has already been mentioned before.

The greatest monument that he has left for mankind is the "*Ramakrishna Mission*" which developed from a humble origin in Baranagore Math into a World Organisation which has taken as its motto—*Love of Mankind and Service to Mankind* without any distinction of caste, creed or colour.

The basic consideration which led to the establishment of this organisation lies in Vivekananda's full and fault-less realisation of *Oneness of human existence.* Every man he regarded as a part of God. So to love man is to love and worship God. Vivekananda's love of God, therefore, flowed into a love of man. With Vivekananda Dharma meant Karma. 'Work is worship'—

was his motto. Work, however, must be *Niskama Karma,* which in its ultimate analysis means disinterested 'Seva' to humanity.

Vivekananda's message to mankind contains three cardinal principles:

First—Equality of all religious faiths which are different ways (paths) of reaching him.

Secondly—Oneness of human existence—Every human being is a part of God. So to love man is to love God.

Thirdly—'Seva', that is to say disinterested service for the good of humanity, means worship of God. So, through Karma one can realise God.

He *regarded all religions as equal.* That is why in his response to the welcome accorded at Chicago, while addressing the Sisters and Brothers of America, Swamiji said that we believe not only in universal toleration, but *we accept all religions as true.*

I am proud to belong to a nation which has sheltered the persecuted and the refugees of all religions and all nations of the earth[2]. *Thus, according to him all religions were equal and equally true. M. Romain Rolland in his excellent monograph on Vivekananda has quoted the savant to say as follows: "After long study and experience, I have come to these conclusions, that:*

1. *All religions—(and by that, I, the author, personally understand those of reason as well as of faith) are true.*
2. *All religions have some error in them.*
3. *All religions are almost as dear to me as my own Hinduism. My veneration for other faiths is the same as for my own faiths.*[3] *It is no wonder that a personality inspired by the values of reason and freedom should advocate a Universal religion.*

"What is religion? Religion has been defined variously. Mahabharata says that religion is that which sustains the social structure[4]. Religion is the means to attain the material as well as the spiritual advancement says the Vaisesika Darsan[5]".

According to Vivekananda religion means so many attempts of the human soul to grasp and realise the infinite[6]. Get rid, in the first place, of all these limited ideas and see God in every person working through all hands, walking through all feet, and eating through every mouth. In every being He lives, through all minds He thinks He is self-evident, nearer unto us than ourselves. To know this, is religion, is faith[7].

There are two theories about the genesis of religion. One theory is to the effect that the ancestor-worship marks the beginning of religious ideas. This is know as the Spirit theory of religion. The other theory of religion is that religion originates in the personification of the powers of nature. This theory is known as the Evolution of the Infinite. Having regard to the ancient religions of the Egyptians, Babylonians, Chinese, and many other races in America and elsewhere, Swamiji accepted the Spirit theory of religion. But whatever may be the beginning of religion , its end is common to all religions, namely, to know one's Creator and to see him in every fellow- being. It is out of this sense of oneness of the end of all religions that the idea of a Universal religion might have occurred to Vivekananda.

Vivekananda's master, Sri Ramakrishna, says that knowledge leads to unity, ignorance to diversity. To realise the infinite or God is the mission of human life. According to the master many are the names of God and infinite the forms that lead us to know Him. In whichsoever name or from you desire to call Him in that very form and name, you will see Him[8]. Being permeated with such catholic outlook, Vivekananda advocated a Universal religion, free any dogma.

It will be seen that religion is highest plane of human though and life. It is said about war that war brings out the best and the worst in man. The same remark applies to religion. Religion begets the most intense love and breeds the bitterest hatred. Religion is like fire, it can burn a Latimer alive or can as well convey oblations to the heavenly gods for human welfare. Religion can thus be a divine or a hell-fire. More blood is shed in the name of religion in human history, than even in the heat of imperialism. That is why there is greater need for religious tolerance, nay for the integration of all religions.

Generally speaking we find a certain number of fanatics in every religion. Swamiji calls fanaticism as a disease of the human brain. It is one of the worst diseases at that. Swamiji was very proud of the absence of fanaticism in India. Indians believe in the Vedic faith of universality that which exists is one. Sages call it by various names! India is the only country where there never has been religious persecution, where never was any man disturbed or his religious faith. Theists or atheists, monists, dualists or nonotheists are there, and they always lived unmolested. Materialists were allowed to preach from the steps of Brahmanical temples, against the gods, and against God Himself; they went preaching all over the land that the idea of God was a mere supersitions and that gods and Vedas, and religion were simply superstitions invented by the priests for their own benefit, and they were allowed to do this unmolested.[9] India's tolerant attitude is thus well-known Religion in India forms the pivot of life. Vivekananda says: "In India religious life forms the centre, the key-note of the whole music of national life: and if any nation attempts to throw off its national vitality, the direction which has become its own through transmission, of centuries, that nation dies, if it succeeds in the attempt. Our life blood of spirituality. If it flows clear, pure and vigorous, everything is fight; political, social, any other material defect even the poverty of the land will be all cured if that blood is pure[10]".

Universal brotherhood is the fountain-head of a universal religion. In every religion there are three essential aspects, philosophical, mythological and ritualiastic. Philosophy expounds the basic principles of religion and its goal and the means to reach it. Mythology consists of the legends that have gathered round the religious beliefs of the people. Ritual of a religion is the *Acara Dharma.* It often gains prominence as the common masses attach ore importance to the concrete manifestations of a religion expressed through the ritual. That you have to fast or feast on a particular day is a part of the ritual. Even a Gyani has to follow ritual in order not to set a bad example to the laity. The "Gita" calls it the doctrine of *Lokasangraha.*

The universal feature common to all religions is the pursuit of the divinity. Unity in variety is the plan of the universe 'many', God is one . Thus, variety being the innate nature of the universe, Vivekananda says that by the ideal of a universal religion does mean a universal philosophy, or universal mythology a universal ritual. Swamiji's faith was that truth is like the Sun. It can be expressed in a hundred thousand ways, and each of these ways is true so for as it goes and hence he was keen to formulate a harmonious religious creed to make all religions come together in love.

Knowledge, devotion, renunciation and action are the four well known paths to attain Godhood. These paths represent the philosophical, the emotional, the mystic and the active types of human beings. So a universal religion must necessarily satisfy all these four types of minds. A perfect man has according to Vivekananda all these sides. Says he: "To become harmoniously balanced in all these four directions, is my ideal of religion. And this religion is attained by what we, in India, Yoga-Union[11]".

Thus the perfect man must be something of a 'Gyana-Yogin', 'Bhakti-Yogin', 'Raj-Yogin and a 'Karma-Yogin'. The 'Gyana-Yogin', the philosopher, the thinker wants to attain the infinite through knowledge i.e. through metaphysics. His soul yearns to see the transcenden reality beyond the visible universe. Swamiji has observed: "He whom I have described to you as the Life of this universe as present as present in the atom and in the suns and moons, He is the basis of our own life, the soul of our soul. Nay, thou art That". This is what *Gyana-Yoga* teaches. If shows to mankind the real unity of being, and that each one of us is the Lord God himself.

The 'Bhakti-Yogin' is the emotional type, the lover of God. It is a selfless love expecting nothing in return. Love is an end in itself.

A 'Raja-Yogin' is the psychological Yogin, the mystic. He believes in acquiring knowledge of the infinite through concentration. Even the lowest shoeblack, if he gives more concentration, will blacken shoes better. Human mind is charged with thousands of undesirable impulses and thoughts. How to check them and bring them under control is in the ambit to 'Raja-Yoga'.

The 'Karma-Yogin' attains God through continuous work and action, without a desire for fruit. It is being like a lotus leaf in the waterpond.

Religion is realisation, not talk nor doctrine nor theory, however beautiful they may be. Prof. R.D. Ranade also shares this ideas of religion being self- realisation. "It is being and becoming, not having or acknowledging, but, it is the entire soul become changed into what it believes. That is religion."

This is ideal of universal religion preached by Vivekananda. A man can attain perfection through the practice of these Yogas or paths to divinity, to whatever religion he may belong. This the highest common multiple of all religions. Swamiji has observed that—If the Parliament of Religions has shown anything to the world it is this: "It has proved to the world that holiness, purity and charity are not the exclusive possession of any church in the world, and that every system has produced men and women of the most exalted character." Vivekananda not only preached but he also practised this universal religion of a Vedantist. He himself was an embodiment of this universal religion.

Efforts were made in the history of India , Alexandria, Europe, Japan, Tibet and also in America for formulating a universal religion—or creed. It is a grand ideal indeed, through a distant one. For the advancement of it, Vivekananda established the Vedant Society in New York in 1896, and other missions.

Dreamers also have a place in the fortune of mankind Mr. Wendell Wilkie advocated the theory One World'. Vivekananda preached for universal religion based on universal brotherhood and fellow-feeling which he stressed while addressing the delegates to the Chicago Parliament of Religions as, 'Sisters and Brothers.' A Utopia is the blue print of human progress. It may be called a century-plan for humanity. "The saints are the heralds of the superman," said Prof. Toynbee, "We hope for the day when the dream of man to have a universal, integrated path of material and spiritual progress may be agreed upon and pursued by man in his collective". Right had Vivekananda to preach the lofty ideal of universal religion? The answer is given by Prof. Wright of the University of Harvard in these memorable words: "To ask you, Swamiji, for your credentials is like asking the sun to state its rights to shine[13]."

M. Romain Rolland has eloquently observed that "A great voice is made to fill the sky. The whole earth is its sounding box. ... Vivekananda appeared in spite of himself as an emperor, whose aim was to discipline the independent but coordinate kingdoms of the spirit under the sceptre of the One. And the world which he founded has proceeded according to this plan."

REFERENCES

1. Vivekananda, Study of Religion, p. 50.
2. Chicago Addresses, p. 2.
3. Romain Rolland, Life of Vivekananda, p. 339.
4. धारणात् धर्ममित्याहुः ।
5. यतोऽभ्युदयनिश्रेयस् सिद्धिः स धर्मः ।
6. Study of Religion, p. 213.
7. Study of Religion, pp. 17-18.
8. Thus Spoke Ramkrishna, pp. 1-2.
9. Study of Religion, pp. 187-88.
10. Vidyarthi, India's Culture Through the Age, p. 362.
11. Study of Religion, p. 108.
12. *Ibid*, pp. 123- 124.
13. Teachings of Vivekananda, Introduction, p. X.

3

Bases of Vivekananda's Educational Thought

Vivekananda's educational ideas been influenced by three major factors: (1) Love for his Master, (2) Love for the nation, and (3) Personal convictions.

Love for his Master

Sri Ramakrishna was the grand ideal of his life. His only mission was to preach the gospel of his Guru (Master) who made him what he was. While Ramakrishna had preached his sermons in great simplicity, through stories and parable, Vivekananda expounded them with the eloquence of a religious teacher in a more modern and logical way. "He verified the truth of his Master's message with a firm conviction born of his own realization: he presented before the world the precious lessons he had learnt at the feet of Ramakrishna.."

Vivekananda used to say that his Master was actually a living illustration of the great upanishadic declarations. In the life of Mother Sarada Devi, he saw the grand ideal of Indian women-hood. He found in her the strength of purity and chastity to stand the test of lust and passion. She perfected in herself the best in Indian culture and Sri Ramakrishna set the best example of how a husband should treat his wife. Perhaps he wanted her to become the Mother of the masses.

Vivekananda saw in his great Guru the whole of religion, the whole of the Upanishads and the vedas. He said "Sri Ramakrishna was the living commentary to the Vedas and their aim."[2] He could experience the real power of the inner man, the 'Atman', by a single touch of his master, which electrified him and made him. God-conscious throughout his life. So naturally, in all his utterances there is a strong note of spirituality which has its roots in the heart of India.

Selfless service was Sri Ramakrishna's 'life principle'. He gave the correct vision of the 'Gita' the Absolute could be know by the path of Karma-Yoga. He taught that selfless devotion to duty is the them of the Gita. When Arjuna was in a dilemma, Krishna gave His vision, and it was enough for Arjuna to act. Similarly Sri Ramakrishna wanted Vivekananda to carry out his mission and he did it in a selfless manner. Sister Nivedita says, "Sri Ramakrishna, as I think, provided basis and sanction for what was to be predominant thought with his great disciple."[3]

Vivekananda was a real Karma- yoga and was not a mere ascetic following only the path of Jnana-Yoga. He was dedicated to his work with a sense of renunciation thereby setting anew example in the order of Sanyasins in modern India.

One great innovation which Vivekananda introduced in the Ramakrishna Mission was compulsory social service which every novice must do before becoming a monk. It seems Vivekananda got this idea from the Christian mission working in America though the same had its origin in India in the days of the Buddha.

Vivekananda found in Sri Ramakrishna the proper answer to every question regarding idol worship, incarnation, dualism and the like. Vivekananda alone knew the manifold and varied excellences of his Guru. In the personality of Sri Ramakrishna, so Vivekananda believed, one could find a glowing and tangible demonstration of India's spirituality and Indian history. "Sri Ramakrishna "says Romain Rolland, "was the consummation of two thousand years of spirituality of three hundred million people."[4] Though Vivekananda was very original in his thinking and propositions, he always said in all humility that he was simply restating his master's message throughout. As a matter of fact, the spiritually rooted sociological doctrines of Sri Ramakrishna and Vivekananda, with their stress on cultivation of purity and strength, have been the restatement of the perennial philosophy of justice, love and universal compassion—which existed in ancient India.

Vivekananda always said that the path of spirituality lay in the material and social upliftment of the masses. To this end he was able to make out the Vedanta a social philosophy which could work well in India through a man making education. While he felt proud of India's past glory and rich spiritual heritage, he was deeply moved to see her in poverty, tyranny and oppression during his life time.

Love for the Nation

Vivekananda was one of the greatest exponents of Indian nationalism in the 19th century. He vehemently criticised the social stratification of Indian society on the basis of caste, power or position.

Like Hegel, Vivekananda believed that there must be one dominating principle manifesting itself in life of every nation. To him religion had been the guiding principle of everything in Indian history. He was a passionate advocate of the religious theory of nationalism because he thought that religion should be the backbone of Indian national life. He believed that the future greatness of a nation could be built only on the foundations of its past greatness. Vivekananda did a significant service to Indian politics by pleading for a religious and spiritual approach to nationalism. He was actually a champion of India's right of self-determination. He was much against the meaningless social stratification. He was much against the meaningless social stratifications of his time which resulted in a kind of social tyranny. He taught the people of India to develop freedom of thought and action and freedom of conscience. He believed that freedom could be attained only through the recognition of interdependence of all human beings. As a nationalist leader, Vivekananda stood for the liberation of the whole of mankind and not for a particular section of society.

Vivekananda's concepts of nationalism and freedom represent a synthesis o eastern and western concepts. He was always against the subject centred British system of education in India which ignored the fundamental aspirations of the country. He emphasised that all educational reforms should be based on India's cultural heritage and national ideals. The same view was held by Percy Nunn when he said "Educational ideas are correlative to the ideals of life."[5]

In the complete works of Vivekananda, one can find his vision of a 'New India' in which the spirit of equality, social awareness and practical efficiency of the 'Modern West' would get happily blended with the nature of gentleness and tolerance of Indian tradition. His great message of nation building is chiefly based on spirituality and her age old ways of life, she would perish. He says, "This is the motherland of philosophy, of spiritually and of ethics, sweetness, gentleness and love and India is still the first and foremost of all the nations of the world in these respects."[6]

Vivekananda was not a visionary who spent all his life in contemplation and meditation. He was extremely sensitive person who reacted with great intensity when there was need to defend the cause of his mother country. His political philosophy contained in itself all vigour and enthusiasm as reflected in his *Lectures from Colombo to Almora, The East and the West and Modern India.*

Like Rousseau he believed in the natural rights of man. Vast powers are placed in the hands of man. But they are to be guided by the power of his heart through amoral and spiritual discipline. Indian thought recognises no compartments and divisions in the human personality leading to mutual exclusion. Man loses his life's battle when he fails to find out his divine nature. The awareness of the inner self is the priceless contribution of India to the world and the future of India largely depends upon continuing this great contribution to humanity.

India's mission to the is to instil in the minds of the people the spirit of tolerance and love, and this can be possible only with the resurrection of values of human life based on the vedantic ideals which existed in ancient times. So it is on the strength of the vedantic ideals that Vivekananda wants a new system of education for India.

Personal Convictions

Vivekananda believed that "all soul elevating ideas and the different branches of knowledge that exist in the world are found on proper investigation, to have their roots in India."[7] To him, a nation that has no history of its own has nothing in this world. The history of India is the history of great seers of the past. India is a land of religion and her message to the world is religious toleration and universal brotherhood.

As a widely travelled teacher throughout India and a large part of the western world, vivekananda could gain first hand knowledge and experience about the miseries of the masses and deterioration of value of human life. In India he found the upper classes exploiting the weaker sections in the name of racial purity. The entire society was saturated with superstitions and caste distinctions. Education was considered the privilege of a few who never wanted to consider the common masses. They were fascinated mainly by the commercial fetishes of the West and were least bothered about national integration or economic equality.

In the West, Swamiji noted that the people were prepared to undertake any hard task for national advancement and economic progress. They had great faith in themselves and they could create history. They worked for just and equitable distribution of wealth. They liked to preserve political independence and national character as sacred ideals. In matters of wealth and health the West appeared far superior to the East. But he strongly felt that the West had much to learn from the East, specially spirituality.

Vivekananda was an ardent patriot and was an embodiment of courage and freedom. He had identified himself with the country and its historic ideals. At the same time he had no hesitation in adapting anything from the West that would be of real use to India. He never entertained the idea of narrow nationalism or narrow sectarian outlook. He had a Catholic and tolerant mind and discovered the fundamental unity behind all the nations of the world. Nehru says "His was a kind of nationalism which automatically slipped into Indian nationalism which was part of internationalism.

In Swamiji's view renunciation and service must continue to be the grand ideals if India and the educational system must give maximum importance to the growth of three major faculties, viz : (1) heart, (2) will, (3) love of truth. To him the present system required thorough overhauling; due attention must be paid to physical strength, practical aptitude, economic efficiency, cultural integrity and training of the will and emotions.

Reconstruction of Modern India

Vivekananda was convinced of the fact that Indian society was facing a very great cultural crisis in his time. Lock of faith in India's ancient ideals on the one hand and terrible economic pressure on the other had created a sense of confusion and chaos within the society. Many social evils like priest- craft, untouchability, poverty, ignorance, superstition, etc., had also their due share in making the counter totally weak.

Vivekananda took it as life's mission to find out a permanent solution to the prevailing problems of his time. He saw with his mental eyes that the masses should be made conscious of their rights and responsibilities through a sound system of education. In his eyes, majority of the politicians were opportunists and so he wanted to recruit a set of social workers to undertake this great task with a sense of commitment.

Vivekananda tried his best to kindle in the minds of the people of India the need for having a national awakening. In his days the people were politically divided. They never thought of the nation and were interested only in the attainment of selfish end. Vivekananda took great pains to travels throughout the country for uniting the scattered races and wanted them to think of India as a whole.

He believed that by uniting 'karma' with 'religion' he could enlighten the people to think of religion in the right way. He appreciated the West for their programmes in science but criticised them for science should benefit all the people of the world.

Swami Vivekananda made his spiritual energy into a powerful lever for lifting India out of priest craft and social tyranny and reaped double advantage through his visit to the western countries. First, he drew the attention of the West to Indian civilization and to the definite aim of religion. Secondly he gave India fresh grounds for his country, Vivekananda became the prophet of a new integral nationalism in India.

India in the latter half of the 19th century witnessed the growth of science and technology, just as all over the world, and this threatened the very base of her spiritual and cultural development. Man's faith in God was severely shaken and it brought about a social and moral devaluation in the country in the country. The Indian intellectuals were so dazzled by western civilization that they began to imitate the West without examining whether it would suit their innate qualities and interests. Consequently Vivekananda wanted a spiritual re-orientation of social, political and economic attitudes of the people. He said that the great scriptures of the Vedas, the upanishads and the Gita contained in them the secrets of spiritual wisdom which would serve for the liberation of India.

Vivekananda thus championed the championed the cause of social harmony and unity in modern India. He taught his countrymen that they should have faith in themselves. He not only stood for spiritual freedom but also wanted the external freedom of man. Instead of talking about political freedom and social justice, he talked about the concept of strength and fearlessness. He justified his theory of fearlessness on the grounds of philosophic vedantism. He believed that this strength must come to the nation through education. His metaphysics, his philosophy of history and culture and his concepts of nationalism, humanism, tolerance and freedom represent a fine synthesis of eastern and western ideals. His thought-currents were working great miracles in the minds of his contemporaries like Dayananda, Tilak and Tagore.

Re- orientation of Science and Technique of Religion

The outstanding legacy of Vivekananda was that he reconciled life and religion. He upheld that a strong and lasting nationalism could be built in India only on a religious basis. Religion signified to him the eternal principles of life and death and of spiritual progress. In India, Swamiji had discovered a mighty spiritual potential and believed intensely that the country would become vitalised if the masses were made aware of this spirituality. To him the ever-widening split between science and religion had resulted in an intellectual crisis which was highly prejudicial to the growth of mankind. He was convinced beyond doubt that the highly potent psychic energy in man was responsible for all the inventions and discoveries and hence there could be no antithesis between religion and science. Religion is self-culture and self-culture is true education.

Swamiji held that there would not be any limits to the possibilities of knowledge that could be imparted through the medium of religion. He hoped that the schools and colleges would work for the cultivation of fundamental ethics. Each man may choose a particular religion or a particular way for God-realisation, and therefore. There could not be a systematic religious instruction in educational institutions. Religious teaching in denominational schools may lead to more and more religion differences in a country already saturated with religion. He believed that there were common elements in every religion and so fundamental ethics of human life could be taught to the children. The training of the soul, he had know from his master and by his own experience, could not be worked out by reading of books. It should be imparted by the teacher showing a model by living a spiritual life.

To Vivekananda, all religions are different forces in the

economy of God, working for the good of mankind. The principal aim of education is universal brotherhood of man through mutual love and respect. Though the ways appear to be different, all religion have the same destination. The Indian ideal of religion is toleration and acceptance of all sister religions. Unity in variety is the plan of the universe and religion alone can lead mankind to that unity. Education in the right line will lead man to the true sense of religion and help him to acquire knowledge about the perishable nature of human body and the eternity of the soul within it. Thus Vivekananda relates education with religion and suggests, the techniques of self-religion through 'Raja-Yoga' and such other methods.

The Bases of Modern Education

Vivekananda felt that modern education all over world has so far concentrated on 'the learning to do' aspect and not on the 'learning to be' faculties of education. In projecting this view he seems to have been influenced by Sri Saṅkara's thought that education meant transmission of knowledge from the knowledge to future generations. "For only when knowledge is firmly grasped it conduces to one's own good and become capable of transmission."[9]

Vivekananda's philosophy of education is based on universal principles of morality and ethics. Speaking about ultimate value of education, he says that it must focus on the requirement of the human mind. Education keeps the soul in the environment in which it would it would develop well. It initiates the citizen into the spiritual life the nation. It means by which the principle of justice is maintained.

In suggesting a philosophy of education for India, Vivekananda follows the inspiring doctrine of Christ that man must finnd the divine in himself. Idealistic education from the days of Socrates has recognised that education must be directed toward the development of chracter and personality. Plato's philosophy of education was built on the four pillars of worth, wisdom, service and leadership. But it is typical of Plato that "he makes no provision for the education of the lowest classes."

Vivekananda on the other hand, wanted to teach the common masses of India the ideals of synthesis, tolerance and universal harmony.

Vivekananda uses the term Brahman or Atman to mean Truth or Reality. Brahman is synonymous with God. To him, the growth of the 'Atman, must become the cardinal virtue of all educative process. This is possible through a living faith in the great message of the Vedas. To him morality implies conscious, deliberate action for the good of humanity. His doctrine of 'karma' implies freedom of action. So his educational philosophy is a combination of knowledge and action.

In Vivekananda's educational philosophy, the general and special aims of education have a single function of enriching the pupil's personality. Mere book learning is of little use in real life. One must read books, but along with that, ideas are to be properly assimilated in a scientific manner. Here he agrees with the opinion of Erasmus that "it would lead man towards knowledge, honesty and independent judgment."

In answer to the present problems of India he pleads for the creation of a philosophy which gives equal importance to the claims of spirit and matter. To him diversity is as real as unity. Matter is only 'veiled spirit' .Thus he creates a metaphysical synthesis reconciling the claims of spirit and matter, and makes it one of the chief bases of his philosophy of education.

The Powers of the Human Mind

The modern educationists in advanced countries of the West believe that the child's brain is a highly delicate organ, and therefore, requires very careful handling and that the teacher's business consists solely in helping the natural unfoldment of its latent potentialities. They are also unanimous that the syllabus and methods should conform to the psychological requirements of the pupils.

Psychologists like Jung, Spranger and others have pointed out that individuals can be grouped into several personality types in accordance with their usual behaviour patterns. But Vivekananda has gone deep into the very structure of the mind and suggested the means of controlling it for the attainment of real knowledge.

The Importance of 'Yoga' in Education

Vivekananda wants to place maximum emphasis on concentration and meditation in the teaching –learning process. In the practice of Yoga as it is the practice general education, five elements are necessarily involved –the teacher, the taught the aim, the subject and the method. Most of the educational institutions conveniently forget these important elements and keep their students completely separated from the facts of life. Vivekananda stresses that there should be perfect harmony between the inner and outer life of the teacher and he should teach what the student needs and not otherwise. He is convinced of the fact that all knowledge is in the human mind and that the same can be experienced by practising concentration and meditation.

A scientist concentrates his mind and invents many things. Through concentration he opens the layers of the gross mind and penetrates deeply into the higher realms of the mind and gets deeper knowledge. He concentrates all the energies of his mind into one focus and throws them out upon the materials he is analysing and so finds out their secrets.

It is easy to fasten the mind to an object which the mind likes best. Attention and interest are the gate-ways to concentration. All greatmen of the world who have reached high positions in society have practised this idea. Says Swami Sivananda " concentration of the mind on God after purification can give you real happiness and knowledge." The educational idea behind concentration or meditation, is that it leads to intuition for studying things. Dr. S. Radhakrishnan says, "Intuition is the result of a long and arduous process of study and analysis." To Vivekananda it is the essence of personality-development. Freud, the great psycho-analyst of the world, who considered the Libido or sex instinct as the driving force of all human activities only reached the conclusion that man's ultimate desire would be to meet death. Vivekananda's philosophy and psychology of concentration and meditation, on the contrary, make every human being believe that he is a divine spark born out of the Supreme Soul and the ultimate end is to merge with that Supreme Soul or God.

The Ideal Teacher

In his opinion the ideal teacher is one who can initiate his students to practise the essential virtues of 'Brahmacharya' and 'Shraddha' and help them to attain or experience the divinity in them. The teacher is like a father to them and is accorded even more respect than the earthly father for "he gives the pupil his spiritual birth and shows him the way to eternal life." In ancient and medieval India teachers were normally men of renunciation. A teacher must essentially be like a doctor who understands the nature of his student and must know the proper method to tackle him in the best manner possible. He must possess academic brilliance, real aptitude for the profession and necessary teaching skills. The teacher today professes to have knowledge which he collects from the books and periodicals. He uses it in a way that will bring maximum results. The days have gone when the experience of the teacher counted much. Once he was wanted everywhere for what he was and what he stood for. Today he is a mere label in the field of education. The teacher in modern days changes himself instead of trying to change his disciples.

Transmission of Knowledge

To Vivekananda, all teaching implies giving and taking; the teacher gives and the student receives. Here he stresses the need for effective participation in the teaching-learning process. In spiritual sciences the teacher takes the role of the transmitter with immense energy like that of Sri Ramakrishna. Education must not be mere acquisition of factual information from text books; it must create in the learner the right attitude towards his life and positive values for the good of society. Teacher should motivate the students to acquire knowledge and develop in them scientific temper, secular outlook and civic responsibility.

Virtues of a Student

Swamiji suggests that every student should practise the most essential virtues like 'Vivek', or discrimination, between one and the other, 'Vairagya', or determination, etc., because all these are required for a proper realisation of the innerself. But much against Vivekananda's ideal, the present student is a more or less trade unionist, political agitator and anarchist. The so-called political leaders and social reformers have practically failed to harness student power for the attainment of social harmony and well-being. When culture is counted in terms of all other things except values, things must go wrong with education. Money, power and position may have their legitimate places in life, but only the right education can give them the right place in life. Really how the student lives outside the classroom must be considered for evaluation of his educational achievement.

Learning through Activity

Vivekananda anticipated many modern thinkers in suggesting that learning through activity should be the guiding principle of any scheme of education. He wanted every activity in Indian schools and colleges—dance, drama, singing, story telling etc.—in the spirit of the Ramayana and the Mahabharata which will give the students a liking for imbiding the spiritual culture of India. Other activities may include inter-school and inter-collegiate discussions, excursions, camps, first aid squads and the like which will enable the students learn how to sacrifice personal and selfish interests for the sake of the larger interests of society.

Medium of Instruction and Examination

Even after a lapse of nearly four decades after independence, the Indian education system hinges on having a foreign language as the medium of instruction. This is a serious handicap when the compared to other advanced nations. It is a psychological necessity that students should be permitted to learn their lessons through the mother-tongue. But Vivekananda was not very much against English education, especially in college classes. Writing to Alasinge Perumal of Madras in the year 1895 Swamiji expressed his desire thus "We must have a college in Madras to search comparative religions, Sanskrit, the different schools of Vedanta and some European languages." He stressed very much that the practice continuous assessment of the student must be introduced.

REFERENCES

1. Swami Nirvedanand, Shri Ramkrishna and spiritual Renaissance, Ramkrishna Mission Institute of Culture, Calcutta, 1940, p. 174.
2. Eastern and Western Disciples, The Life of Swami Vivekananda, Advaita Ashram, Almora, 1940, p. 52.
3. Sister Nivedita, The Master as I Saw Him, Udhodhan Office, Calcutta, 1972, p. 227.
4. Romain Rolland, Life of Shri Ramkrishna, Advaita Ashram, Almora, 1974, p. 14.
5. Percy Nunn, Education: Its Data and First Principles, London Arnold, 1948, p. 9.
6. Complete Works of Swami Vivekananda, Vol. III, p. 147.
7. *Ibid.*, Vol. V, p. 368.
8. Jawaharlal Nehru, Shri Ramrkishna and Swami Vivekananda, Calcutta Advaita Ashrama, 1976, p. 12.
9. Jagadananda Swami, A Thousand Teachings of Shri Shankaracharya, Mylapore, Shri Ramkrishna Math, 1943, p. 3.

4

What Education Means to Swami Vivekananda

Knowledge—Inherent in Man

What we say a man 'knows', should, in strict psychological language, be what he 'discovers' or 'unveils'; what a man 'learns' is really what he 'discovers', by taking the cover off his own soul, which is mine of infinite knowledge.

We say Newton discovered gravitation. Was it sitting anywhere in a corner waiting for him? It was in his own mind; the time came and he found it out. All knowledge that the world has ever received comes from the mind; the infinite library of the universe is in your own mind. The external world is simply the suggestion, the occasion, which sets you to study your own mind, but the object of your study is always your own mind. The falling of an apple gave the suggestion to Newton, and he studied his own mind. He rearranged all the previous links of thought in his mind and discovered a new link among them, which we call the law of gravitation. It was not in the apple nor in anything in the centre of the earth.

All knowledge, therefore, secular or spiritual, is in the human mind. In many cases it is not discovered, but remains covered, and when the covering is being slowly taken off, we say, 'We are learning', and the advance of knowledge is made by the advance of this process of uncovering. The man from whom this veil is being lifted is the more knowing man, the man upon whom it lies thick is ignorant, and the man from whom it has entirely gone is all-knowing, omniscient. There have been omniscient men, and, I believe, there will be yet; and that there will be myriads of them in the cycles to come.[1]

The Essence of Education

Education is the manifestation of the perfection already in man... . Therefore the only duty of the teacher ... is to remove all obstructions from the way.[2]

The true education, however, is not yet conceived of amongst us... I never define anything.... Still, it may be described as a development of faculty, not an accumulation of words, or as a training of individuals to will rightly and efficiently.[3]

The huge steamer, the mighty railway engine—they are non-intelligent, they move, turn and run; but they are without intelligence. And yonder tiny worm which moved away from the railway line to save its life, why is it intelligent? There is no manifestation of will in the machine, the machine never wishes to transgress law; the worm wants to oppose law, rises against law whether it succeeds or not, therefore it is intelligent. Greater is the happiness, higher is the Jiva, in proportion as this will is more successfully manifest. The will of God is perfectly fruitful, therefore He is the highest.

What is education? Is it book-learning? No. Is it diverse knowledge? Not even that. The training by which the current and expression of will are brought under control and become fruitful is called education. Now consider, is that education as a result of which the will, being continuously choked by force through generations, is well-nigh killed out; is that education under whose sway even the old ideas, let alone the new ones, are disappearing one by one; is that education which is slowly making man a machine? It is more blessed, in my opinion, even to go wrong impelled by one's free will and intelligence than to be good as an automation.[4]

Education is not filling the mind with a lot of facts. Perfecting the instrument and getting complete mastery of my own mind [is the ideal of education].[5]

To me the very essence of education is concentration of mind, not the collecting of facts. If I had to do my education over again, and had any voice in the matter, I would not study facts at all. I would develop the power of concentration and detachment, and then with a perfect instrument I could collect facts at will. Side by side, in the child, should be developed the power of concentration and detachment.[6]

Education is not the amount of information that is put into your brain and runs riot there, undigested, all your life. We must have life-building, man-marking, character-making assimilation of ideas. If you have assimilated five ideas and made them your life and character, you have more education than any man who has got by heart a whole library ....If education is identical with information, the libraries are the greatest sages in the world, and encyclopaedias are the Rishis.[7]

We want that education by which character is formed, strength of mind is increased, the intellect is expanded, and by which one can stand on one's own feet.[8]

The education which does not help the common mass of people to equip themselves for the struggle for life, which does not bring out strength of character, a spirit of philanthropy, and the courage of a lion—is it worth the name? Real education is that which enables one to stand on one's own legs.[9]

Another things that we want is the abolition of that system which aims at education our boys in the same manner as that of the man who battered his ass, being advised that it could thereby be turned into a horse…no one can teach anybody. The teacher spoils everything by thinking that he is teaching. Thus Vedanta says that within man is all knowledge—even in a boy it is so and it requires only an awakening and that much is the work of a teacher. We have to do only so much the boys that they may learn to apply their own intellect to the proper use of their hands, legs, ears, eyes, etc. and finally everything will become easy.[10]

Hands off ! as I always say, and everything will be right. That is our duty is to clear the way.[11]

Do not try to disturb the faith of any man. If you can give him something better; if you can, get hold of a man where he stands and give him a push upwards; do so, but do not destroy what he has. The only true teacher is he who can convert himself, as it were, into a thousand persons at a moment's notice. The only true teacher is he who can immediately come down to the level of the student, and transfer his soul to the student's soul and see through the student's eyes and hear through his ears and understand through his mind. Such a teacher can really teach and none else. All these negative, breaking -down, destructive teachers that are in the world, can never do any good.[12]

A Close Personal Contact between the Teacher and the Taught

My ideas of education is personal contact with the teacher – Gurugṛiha-Vasa. Without the personal life of a teacher there would be no education. Take your Universities. What have they done during the fifty years of their existence? They have not produced one original man. They are merely an examining body. The idea of the sacrifice for the common weal is yet developed in our nation.[13]

One should live from his very boyhood with one whose character is like a blazing fire and should have before him a living example of the highest teaching. Mere reading that it is a sin to tell a lie will be of no use. Every boy should be trained to practise absolute Brahmacharya, and then, and then only, faith—Shraddha—will come. Otherwise, why will not one who has no Shraddha speak an untruth? In our country, the imparting of knowledge has always been through men of renunciation… India had all good prospects so long as Tyagis (men of renunciation) used to impart knowledge.[14]

Education and Religion

I look upon religion as the innermost core of education.[15]

The root is religion. Religion is as the rice, and everything else, like the curries. Taking only curries causes indigestion, and so is the case with taking rice along.[16]

After preaching spiritual knowledge, along with it will come that secular knowledge and every other knowledge that you want; but if you attempt to get the secular knowledge without religion, I tell you plainly, vain is your attempt in India it will never have a hold on the pepole.[17]

Swamiji's Plan about Religion-Centred Education

We must have a temple, for with Hindus religion must come first. The, you may say, all sects will quarrel about it. But we will make it a non- sectarian temple, having only 'Om' as the symbol, the greatest symbol of any sect. If there is any sect here which believes that 'Om' ought not to be the symbol, it has no right to call itself Hindu. All will have the right to interpret Hinduism, each one according to his own sect ideas, but we must have a common temple. You have your own images and symbols in other places, but do not quarrel here with those who differ from you. Here should be taught the common grounds of our different sects, and at the same time the different sects should have perfect liberty to come and teach their doctrines, with other sects. Say what you have to say, the world wants it; but world has no time to hear what you think about other people; you can keep that to yourselves.

Secondly, in connection with this temple there should be an institution to train teachers who must go about preaching religion and giving secular education to our people; they must carry both. As we have been already carrying religion from door to door, let us along with it carry secular education also. That can be easily done. Then the work will extend through these bands of teachers and preachers, and gradually we shall have similar temples in other place, until we have covered the whole of India. That is my plan.[18]

Not Negative—Positive Education

We must give the public only positive ideas. Negative thoughts weaken men. Do you not find that where parents are constantly are constantly taxing their sons to read and write, telling them they will never learn anything, and calling them fools and so forth, the latter do actually turn out to be so in many cases? If you speak kind words to boys and encourage them, they are bound to improve in time...If you can give them positive ideas , people will grow up to be men and learn to stand on their own legs. In language and literature, in poetry and the art, in everything we must point,out not the mistakes that people are making in their thoughts and actions, but the way in which they will gradually be able to do these things better. Pointing out mistakes wounds a man's feelings. We have seen how Shri Ramakrishna would encourage even those whom we considered as worthless and change the very course of their lives thereby! His very method of teaching was a unique phenomenon.[19]

In New York I used to observe the Irish colonists come—downtrodden, haggard-looking, destitute of all possessions at home, penniless, and wooden-headed—with their only belongings, a stick and a bundle of rags hanging at the end of it, fright in their steps, alarm in their eyes. A difference spectacle in six months—the man walks upright; his attire is changed. In his eyes and steps there is no more sign of fright. What is the cause? Our Vedanta says that that Irishman was kept surrounded by contempt in his own country—the whole of Nature was telling him with one voice—'Pat, you have no more hope, you were born a slave and will remain so'. Having been thus told from his birth, Pat believed in it and hypnotised hmself that he was very low, and the Brahman in him shrank away. While no sooner had he landed in America then the shout went up on sides—'Pat, you are a man as we are, it is who has done all, a man like you and me can do everythings; have courage! Pat raised his head and saw that it was so, the Brahman within woke up, Nature herself spoke, as it were , 'Arise, awake, etc'. (Kath Up, I/iii/4).

Likewise the education that our boys receive is very negative. The schoolboy learns nothing, but has everything of his own broken down – want of Shraddha (faith) is result. The Shraddha which is the keynote of the Vedas and the Vedanta—the Shraddha which emboldened Nachiketa to face Yama and question him, through which Shraddha this world moves—the annihilation of that Shraddha!.. Therefore are we so near destruction. The remedy now is, the spread of education. First of all, Self-knowledge. I do not mean thereby, matted hair, staff, Kamandalu, and mountain caves which the world suggests. What do I mean then ... Dualist, qualified Monist, Monist, Shaiva, Vaishnava, Shakta, even the Buddhist and the Jain and others—whatever sects have arisen in India are all at one in this respect, that infinite power is latent in this Jivatma (individualised soul);... there is the same Atman in all, difference being only in manifestation ... That power manifests as soon as it gets the opportunity and the right place and time. From the highest God to the meanest grass, the same power is present in all—whether manifested o not. We shall have to call forth that power by going from door to door.

Secondly, along with this, education has to be imparted.[20]

The old institution of 'living with the Guru' and similar similar systems of imparting education are needed. What we want are Western science coupled with Vedanta, Brahmacharya as the guiding motto, and also Shraddha and faith in one's own self.[21]

What we need, ... is to study, independent of foreign control, different branches of the knowledge that is our own, and with it the English language and western science; we need technical education and all that may develop industries so that men, instead of seeking for service, may earn enough to provide fort themselves, and save something against a rainy day.[22]

Not that Education which Inculcates Weakness

I have no objection to dualism in many of its forms. I like most of them, but I have objections to every form of teaching which inculcates weakness. This is the one question I put to every man, woman, or child, when they are in physical, mental, or spiritual training. Are you strong? Do you feel strength?—for I know it is truth alone that gives strength. I know that truth alone gives life, and nothing but going towards reality will make us strong, and none will reach truth until he is strong. Every system, therefore, which weakens the mind, makes one superstitions, makes one mope, makes one desire all sorts of wild impossibilities, mysteries, and superstition, I do not like, because its effect is dangerous. Such systems never bring any good; such things create morbidity in the mind, make it weak, so weak that in course of time it will be almost impossible to receive truth or live upto it.[23]

Self-reliance—Our Goal

All the wealth of the world cannot help one little Indian village if the people are not taught to help themselves. Our work should be mainly *educational,* both moral and intellectual.... Educate the people, so that they may learn to be self-reliant, frugal, and not given to marrying, and thus save themselves from future famine.[24]

Flaws in the Present System

It (present university system) is almost wholly one of defects. Why, it is nothing but a perfect machine for turning out clerks. I would even thank my stars if that were all. But no! See how men are becoming destitute of Shraddha and faith. They assert that the Gita is only an interpolation, and that the vedas are but rustic songs! They like to master every detail concerning things and nations outside of India, but if you ask them, they do not know even the names of their own forefathers upto the seventh generation, not to speak of the fourteenth!...A nation that has no history of its own nothing in this world. Do you believe that one who has such faith and pride as to feel, 'I

---

* Lord Curzon, who took steps to raise the standard of university education so high as to make it very expensive and hence almost inaccessible to boys of the middle classes.

come of noble descent', can ever turn out to be bad? How could that be? That faith in himself would curb his actions and feelings, so much so that he would rather die than commit wrong. So a national history keeps a nation well-restrained and does not allow it to sink so low.... Looking from one standpoint you should rather be grateful to the Victory* for his proposal of reforming the university system, which means practically abolishing higher education; the country will, at least, feel some relief by having breathing time. Goodness gracious! What a fuss and fury about graduating, and after a few days all cools down! And after all that , what is it they learn but that what religion and customs we have are all bad , and what the Westerners have are all good! At last, they cannot keep the wolf form the door ! What does it matter if this higher education remains or goes? It would be better if the people got a little technical education, so that they might find work and earn their bread, instead of dawdling about and crying for service.[25]

The education that you are getting now has some good points, but it has a tremendous disadvantage which is so great that the good things are all weighed down . In the first place it is not a man-making education, it is merely and entirely a negative education. A negative education or any training that is based on negation, is worse than death. The child is taken to school, and the first thing he learns is that his father is a fool, the second thing that all his grandfather is a lunatic, the third thing that all his teachers are hypocrites, the fourth that all the sacred books are lies! By the time he is sixteen he is a mass of negation, lifeless and boneless. And the result is that fifty years of such education has not produced one original man in the three presidencies. Every man of originality that has been produced has been educated elsewhere, and not in this country, or they have gone to the old universities once more to cleanse themselves of superstitions.[26]

Education Can Eradicate Destitution of the Masses

Education, education, education alone! Travelling through many cities of Europe and observing in them the comforts and education of even the poor people, there was brought to my mind the state of our own poor people, and I used to shed tears. What ,made the difference ? Education was the answer I got. Through faith in one's own self, and through faith in one's own self the inherent Brahman is waking up in them, while the Brahman in us is gradually becoming dormant.[27]

How can there be any progress of the country without the spread of education, the dawning of knowledge?... But know for certain that absolutely nothing can be done to improve the state of things, unless there is spread of education first among the women and the masses.... History and the Puranas, housekeeping and the arts, the duties of home-life and principles that make for the development of an ideal character have to be taught with the help of modern science, and the women students must be trained up in ethical and spiritual life.... It is only in the homes of educated and pious mothers that great men are born.[28]

Mass Education

Educate and raise the masses, and thus alone a nation is possible.... The whole defect is here: The real nation who live in cottages have forgotten their manhood, their individuality. Trodden under the foot of the Hindu, Mussalman, or Christian, they have come to think that they are born to be trodden under the foot of everybody who has money enough in his pocket. They are to be given back their lost individuality. They are to be educated.... Our duty is to put the chemicals together, the crystallization will come through God's laws. Lets us put ideas into their heads, and they will do the rest . Now this means educating the masses. Here are these difficulties. A pauper government cannot, will not, do anything ; so no help from that quarter.

Even supposing we are in a position to open schools in each village free, still the poor boys would rather go to the plough to earn their living than come to your school. Neither have we the money, nor can we make them come to education. The problem seems hopeless. I have found a way out. It is this.

If the mountain does not come to Mohammed, Mohammed must go to the mountain. If the poor cannot come to education, education must reach them at the plough, in the factory, everywhere. How? You have seen my brethren. Now I can get hundreds of such, all over India, unselfish, good, and educated. Let these men go from village to village bringing not only religion to the door of everyone but also education. So I have a nucleus of organizing the widows also as instructors to our women.

Now suppose the villagers after their day's work have come to their village and sitting under a tree or somewhere are smoking and talking the time away. Suppose two of these educated Sannyasins get hold of them there and with a camera throw astronomical or other pictures, scenes from different nations, histories, etc. Thus with globes, maps etc. – and all this orally- how much can be done that way.... It is not that the eyes is the only door of knowledge, the ear can do all the same. So they would have ideas and morality and hope for better. Here our work ends. Let them do the rest.[29]

There are thousands of single minded, self sacrificing Sannyasins in our own country, going from village to village, teaching religion. If some of them can be organized as teachers of secular things also, they will go from place to place to place, from door, not only preaching but teaching also. Suppose two of these men go to a village in the evening with a camera, a globe, some maps, etc. They can teach a great deal of astronomy and geography to the ignorant. By telling stories about different nations, they can give the poor a hundreds times more information through the ear than they can get in a lifetime through books.[30]

If there is inequality in nature, still there must be equal chance for all or if greater for some and for some less- the weaker should be given more change than the strong. In other words, a Brahmin is not so much in need of education as a Chandala. If the son of a Brahmin needs one teacher, that of a Chandala needs ten. For, greater help must be given to him whom nature has not endowed with an acute intellect from birth.[31]

Female Education

Religion, arts, science, housekeeping, cooking, sewing, hygiene- the simple essential points in these subjects ought to be taught to our women. It is not good to let them touch novels and fiction.... But only teaching rites of worship won't do; their education must be an eye opener in all matters. Ideal characters must always be presented before the view of the girls to imbue them with a devotion to lofty principles of selflessness. The noble examples of Sita, Savitri, Damayanti, Lilavati, Khana, and Mira should be brought home to their minds, and they should be inspired to mould their own lives in the light of these.[32]

But the truth is that some defect or other or other must creep into that learning or culture which is not founded on a religious basis. But now female education is to be spread with religion as its centre. All other training should be secondary to religion. Religious training, the formation of character and observance of the vow of celibacy- these should be attended to. In the female education which has obtained up till now in India, it is religion that has been made a secondary concern.[33]

Education through Colloquial Language

In our country, owing to all learning being in Sanskrit from the ancient times, there has arisen an immeasurable gulf between the learned and the common folk. All the great personages, from Buddha down to Chaitanya and Ramakrishna, who came for the well- being of the world, taught the common people in the language of the people themselves. Of course, scholarship is an excellent thing; but cannot scholarship be displayed through any other medium than a language that is stiff and unintelligible, that is unnatural and merely artificial? Is there no room for in the spoken language? What is the use of creating an unnatural language to the exclusion of the natural one? Do you not think out your scholastic researches in the language which you are accustomed to speak at home? Why then do you introduce such a queer and unwieldy thing when you proceed to put them in black and white? The language in which you think out philosophy and science in your mind, and argue with others in public- is not that the language for writing philosophy and science? If it is not, how then do you reason out those truths within yourselves and in company of others in that very language? The language in which we naturally express ourselves, in which we communicate our anger, grief, or love, etc.—there cannot be a fitter language than that. We must stick to that idea, that manner of expression, that diction and all. No artificial language can ever have that force, and that brevity and expressiveness, or admit of being given any turn you please, as that spoken language. Language must be made like pure steel—turn and twist it any way you like, it is again the same—it cleaves a rock in twain at one stroke, without its edge being turned. Our language is becoming artificial by imitating the slow and pompous movement—and only that—of Sanskrit. And language is the chief means and index of a nation's progress... . Language is the vehicle of ideas. It is the ideas that are of prime importance, language comes after... language, or art, or music that expresses no meaning and is lifeless is of no good. Now they will understand that the more strength is infused into the national life the more will language art and music etc. become spontaneously instinct with ideas and life. The volume of meaning that a couple of words of everyday use will convey, you may search in vain in two thousand set epithets.[34]

The greatness of a teacher consists in the simplicity of his language.[35]

My ideal of language is my Master's language, most colloquial and yet most expressive.[36]

REFERENCES

1. Complete works, Vol. I, p. 28.
2. Letters of Swami Vivekananda, p. 70, 1976.
3. Complete works, Vol. V, p. 231.
4. Letters, pp. 443—44.
5. Vol. I, p. 510.

6. Vol. VI, pp. 38-39.
7. Vol. III, p. 302.
8. Vol. V, p. 342.
9. Vol. VII, pp. 147-148.
10. Vol. V, p. 366.
11. Letters, p. 70.
12. Vol. IV, p. 183.
13. Vol. V, p. 224.
14. Vol. V, p. 369.
15. Vol. V, p. 231.
16. Vol. V, p. 366.
17. Vol. III, p. 223.
18. Vol. III, pp. 302-303.
19. Vol. VII, pp. 170-171.
20. Letter, pp. 229-230.
21. Vol. V, p. 366.
22. Vol. V, pp. 368-369.
23. Vol. II, p. 201.
24. Vol. VII, p. 504.
25. Vol. V, pp. 364-367.
26. Vol. III, pp. 301-302.
27. Letters, p. 329.
28. Vol. VI, p. 489.
29. Letters, pp. 114-115.
30. Letters, p. 118.
31. *Ibid*, p. 255.
32. Vol. VI, pp. 493-494.
33. Vol. VII, p. 220.
34. Vol. VI, 187-189.
35. Vol. V, p. 106.
36. Vol. V, p. 259.

5
Educational Ideas of Vivekananda

Vivekananda's contributed to educational thought is remarkable for its quality and variety as much as for its quantity. Intellectual excellence and depth of vision of the highest order can be noticed in all his educational ideas which are found scattered here and there as most valuable gems in the treasure houses of Vivekananda literature.

An objective analysis of Vivekananda's works reveals that Vivekananda did not construct any systematic theory of education as such. But it is possible, however, to piece together some of his striking ideas on education and make them useful for educational reconstruction in modern India.

Vivekananda's main problem in life was the social and cultural emancipation of India by preaching the gospel of 'self-realization' through selfless service and hence there is an element of spiritualism, or idealism, in all his educational ideas. As highlighted on the first chapter, he viewed education as the manifestation of perfection already in man. To him, the law of gravitation was already there, in Newton's mind. "The time came and he found it out." Though he was not a realist in the Hobbesian or Machiavallian sense of the term, he was never in his life a pragmatist. His educational ideas in those days represented a synthesis of some of the dominant conceptions of Indian thought and the democratic ideas of the modern West.

The Bases of His Educational Philosophy

Vivekananda was a versatile genius who had mastered the Upanishads, the Mahabharata, the Ramayana, the Bhagavat Gita, the Bible and the Koran, and also the entire western thought from Plato to Spencer. He is said to have mastered the eleven volumes of the *Encyclopaedia Britannica*. He had great respect and admiration for the vedic and vedantic tradition of India represented by Sri Sankara, Ramanuja and Madhva and had the highest and deepest devotion to his master Sri Ramakrishna who taught him the lessons of purity and strength.

To him divinity is as real as unity in diversity. He regards time, space and causation as relevant only to the phenomenal world. "Maya" in this context " is a statement of fact of this universe, of how it is going on." Advaita is his grand ideal and spirituality the divine guidelight. The central concept of Vivekananda's philosophy is the 'Brahman' which means supreme energy. It is the highest reality, knowledge and bliss. He says, "the Brahman is the general cause of all these manifestation." As a widely travelled man of great experience, he was awakened to the significance of scientific advancement and so he pleaded for a "unity between the Indian ideal of contemplation and western ideal mastering external nature."

The great seers of India like Buddha, Sri Sankara and Sri Ramakrishna had done wonderful work to preach the divinity in man. Vivekananda found in Sri Ramakrishna his entire motherland and the people. Vivekananda pleads that in India what is wanted is the re-establishment of spirituality and nothing else. He says, "Before flooding India with sociological or political ideas, first deluge the land with spiritual ideas." He admits that there are some good points in the present system of education but is has tremendous disadvantages and the good things are all weighed down. The English man believes in himself and has that strength to stand on his legs. This belief is yet to come in India though it has been preaching religion all these ages.

Education on National Lines

The first task of education is to make the people of the country strong. "The first Gods we have to worship are our countrymen." Till then there is no salvation for the race. Generally a man considers another man educated only if he can pass some examinations and deliver good lectures. To Vivekananda, the education, which does not help the people to equip themselves for the struggle for life, or which does not bring strength of character, cannot be treated as worth its name. Modern education has changed the fashion of the day. Today the child is taken to school in pomp and glory and the first thing he learns is that his father is a fool. There is no use in keeping this trend. The greatest task of education is to reform the human mind. "The ideal for India, therefore, is that we must have the whole education of our country, spiritual or secular in our own hands and its must be on national lines, through national methods as far as possible. To Vivekananda the dominant theme of Indian history is to find out the underlying unity in diversity. He accepted the immense worth of the spiritual heritage of India and the cultural synthesis it had through ages.

Education is a continuous process. It should cover all aspects of life, physical material, intellectual, emotional, moral and spiritual and all stages of life from birth to death. Moreover, it must meet the needs and problems of men and women in all walks of life. Sri Ramakrishna used to say "As long as I live, so long do I learn." Vivekananda practised this idea throughout his life.

Faith and Strength

Vivekananda says that no good comes out of the man who, day and night, thinks he is weak and miserable. One should always remember that nothing is impossible in this world. The fact is that one becomes what he actually thinks. To him, faith is the only thing which can push forward a nation in the march of civilization. Imitation is not civilization. It is just like an ass in a lion skin. In spite of the greatness of the Upanishads, in spite of the boasted ancestry of the sages, the people of India are yet to understand this principle. "The idea of true "shraddha" must be brought back once more to us, the faith in ourselves must be reawakened."

He also observes that the whole of Indian national character is one of childish independence. The people are brought to believe that they are weak and have no independence in anything. They are ready to enjoy food if it is brought to their mouth. Herein lies India's real weakness. If India wants to survive, its people should have faith in themselves. It is weakness that is the source of all selfishness. If there is weakness there is no patriotism. In India the Upanishads serve as a great mine of strength. He adds "the truths of the Upanishads are before you. Take them up, live up to them and the salvation of India will be at hand."

The Indian Ideal

India is a land of religion and to the Indian mind "Religion is the manifestation of divinity in man." Centuries of education have always been in that line; and the result is that it is the one concern in life. In his opinion religion is the inner-most core of education. Religion is the treasure house of eternal truths and these truths have been realised by the ancient rishis of India.

Religion is the way of the heart. It is the heart which takes one to the highest plane, which intellect can never reach. Temples and churches, books and forms, are simply the kindergarten of religion to make the spiritual child strong enough to take the higher steps. Religion is not in doctrines or dogmas nor in intellectual argumentation. It is actually the heart's possession. "The intensest love that humanity has ever known has come from religion."

In India religion is the nation's soul. Whether it is right or not, the nation is bound by it and so it must be strengthened. Religion is the discipline which touches human conscience; it helps man in his struggle with evil, frees him from greed and saves him from lust and hatred. It is the religious inclination that unifies a society.

To Swamiji religion is not merely based on dogmas, creeds or rites, but has a rational ethical and spiritual philosophy. In the west, tyranny of the wise and priest-craft are not so degenerated as they are in India. Swamiji says, "Stand up and reason out; have no blind faith." It is high time that Indians have assimilated their ancient ideals. They must feel the fragrance of their flowers contained in the Vedanta. "If you have assimilated five ideas and made them your life and character, you have more education than any man who has got by heart a whole library."

Education should be something in the line of positive teaching. Mere book learning won't do for assimilation of ideas. India wants a type of education by which strength of mind is increased and intellect is expanded and by which one can be a real man. "What we want are western science coupled with Vedanta."[1]

All religions except that of India believe that the universe in its entirely is composed of parts separated from each other—God Nature and Man—each stands by itself isolated from another. But in India, education seeks to find unity in the midst of diversity. Everything in India is spiritual and all find expression in religion.

In order to make the country potentially strong with muscles of iron and nerves of steel, it is necessary that the Indian mind should be trained to focus its attention to the highest goal of man-making education. "It is man-making religion that we want. It is man-making theories that we want. It is man-making education all round that we want."

The Psychology of Education

The mind is the fundamental substance which does the entire function in the learning process. That which helps the mind to do this function is concentration. The more the power of concentration, the greater the knowledge that is acquired.

"The very essence of education is concentration of mind." From the lowest man to the highest yogi, all have to use the same method to attain knowledge. All success in any line of work is the result of concentration.

An animal has very little power of concentration. So the main difference between man and animal is in their power of concentration. This difference in the degree of concentration is also found between man and man. The Vedanta says that within man is all knowledge, even in a child it is so and it requires only an awakening and that is the work of the teacher. "The explanation of everything is after all in yourself."

Vivekananda believes that each race in the world has a peculiar bent, a peculiar mission to fulfil in this life. Similarly each individual has his own peculiarities, being a product of heredity and environment. "An individual's life is marked out for him by the infinite past life, by all his past Karma."

Education for Knowledge

The ultimate goal of mankind is the re-union with the divinity which is the true nature of this universe. Education for knowledge is the best means to realise this goal. According to a higher psychological analysis of the advaitists, all these various changes in the world are caused by space, time and causation and are differentiated only by form and name. They say that the same divine nature is present in the lowest worm as well as in the highest human being. The individualised self which tries to be different from all other beings is the main source of all social evils. "When this idea of self has been got rid of, all struggle will cease, all misery vanish." To Vivekananda, the most important among the qualifications required for this kind of knowledge are 'Shama', 'Dama', Shradha', etc,. which may be taken together for keeping the thought currents in the desired way without allowing them to stray out.

The Yoga-way in Education

The science of Yoga claims that it has discovered the laws

with which man can very easily strengthen his power of concentration and meditation. To Vivekananda this is one of the great practical things and this is the secret of all education. In the yoga system, there are impersonal principles that one can practise and find full expansion of his inherent powers. Proper food, exercise, sleep and wakefulness are required for keeping the mind steady, in its pursuit of knowledge. The yoga-way is to keep the body and mind pure and strong for self-development as well as total fulfilment. The teacher should make a careful study of the nature of the trainee and show him the path which suits him best.

The practice of yoga requires a high degree of concentration. In fact all success in any line of work is the result of concentration. As soon as a person tries to concentrate on a particular object of knowledge, thousands of undesired impulses may rush into the brain and consequently disturb the mind. "How to check these impulses and bring the mind under control is the whole subject of study in 'Raja-yoga'." The physical body is the gross part of the mind and so in the training of mind it is easier to reach it through the body. Swamiji is fully convinced that the Yoga-way will help the student to develop his innate qualities like fearlessness, love, sympathy, etc., and equip him to lead an ideal life. It always brings about culture of the human heart.

Education and Experience

Vivekananda believes that all education secular or spiritual is based on experience. Whether it is inductive reasoning or deductive reasoning, experience is the real guide. The first principle of reasoning is that the particular is applied by the general, the general by the more general until one reaches the eternal. Reason is what is wanting in every educated man or woman to apply the discoveries of secular knowledge in the different realms of human experience. If education is to be made meaningful it must be a matter of real experience. He says, "Experience is the one great teacher—experience of pleasure and pain—but know it is only experience. This is to mean that every educated man has to go through different experiences in order to attain real knowledge.

Education and Personality

The great ideal of education is the development of human personality. For this one has to understand for oneself the laws which develop the personality of man and by proper understanding and practice each one can grow and strengthen ones personality. Vivekananda says "This is one of the great practical things and this is the secret of all education." In the life of the householder, in the life of the poor or the rich, there is need for strengthening of personality. According to Vedanta, only a pure moral man has control of his will. This pure moral man who throws his imagination upon his fellow being has nothing to fear, he is a dynamo of power and can do anything and everything in a calm and dispassionate manner. To Swamiji, strength and fearlessness are the two major characteristics of human personality. Strength is goodness, weakness is Sin."[2]

The Real Task of Education

Educationists of the East and the West have time and again presented a wide variety of meaning to the concept of education. But in the absence of an accepted standard, the student of education is tantalized to find out a suitable choice. At the same time, every critical student knows that there are certain objective values of education which are fundamental and eternal like Truth, Beauty and Justice. Disinterested pursuit of any of these values will lead one to the manifestation of perfection of his own self. Education is a misnomer unless it trains the will of man. The real task of education according to Vivekananda is (the training by which the current and expression of the will are brought under control for the benefit of society.

To him, the human will or mind is the infinite library of the universe. A person comes to know of his will when it begins to operate in a given environment. All knowledge the world has ever received comes from the will of man and all discoveries are the result of the activity of the will. Education alone can bring to light the wonderful capacities of the human mind which is a part of the universal mind. Education must, therefore, aim at information of character, strength of mind, expansion of intellect and ability to stand on ones own feet.

The Learning Process

Since the mind is perfect in itself there is no necessity for it to receive knowledge from outside. A simple rearrangement of previous impressions in the mind would lead to new propositions and theories as happened in the case of Sri Isaac Newton who discovered the low of Gravitation.

Learning is, therefore, the process of discover of knowledge within the mind. "Like fire in a piece of flint, knowledge exists in the mind, suggestion is the friction which brings it out."

The impression received by the mind from the external world serves as suggestion for future course of action. "What a man "learns" is what he really 'discovers' by taking the cover off his own soul. Which is a infinite knowledge."

Just as the oak tree is natural to the acorn, so is knowledge to the human mind. Its manifestation is only a question of being conscious of it. So to become conscious of this knowledge is the purpose of all educative propose of all educative.

The nature of the human mind is such that "no one was ever really taught by another; each of us has to be teacher himself."

The external teacher offers only the suggestion and the rest is to be worked out by the internal teacher, the mind within. This is the real spirit of the learning process.

The Teacher and the Taught

Time there was when education was gained by constant living in communion with nature. The great educational institution in the days of the Upanishads, and Nalanda and Taxila in later times were important centuries of learning which shed their light on the true nature of the relationship that existed between the teacher and the taught. Vivekananda says, "without the personal life of the teacher there would be no education."

One of the peculiar aspects of the ancient system was that "the teacher used to take student without charge, and not only so, most of them gave their students food and clothes." To support these teachers the wealthy families made gifts to them. The virtues necessary the taught were purity, a real thirst for knowledge and perseverance. Without faith, humility, submission and veneration towards the teacher, there was no education at all.

Vivekananda has great appreciation for the 'gurugriha vasa'. He suggests that "the charge of imparting knowledge should again fall upon the shoulders of Tyagis." The modern teacher should take the ancient guru as a model and follow his example.

According to Vivekananda no spiritual knowledge is possible so long as the mind is restless and out of control. So he wants the disciple to have great power of endurance. Then only the teacher can come down to the level of the student and transmit knowledge to him. He also wants that "every pupil should be trained to practice absolute Brahmacharya." Brahmacharya is necessary for the development of Shraddha or faith which is the most essential basis of an ideal system.

The essential nature of education is making real use of the 'ideas' and not merely storing of facts by rote memory. He says "Books are useless until our book opens; then all other book are good, so far as they conform to our book." "No one can teach anybody. The teacher spoil everything by thinking that he is teaching."

Man-making Education

Vivekananda says, "Education is not the amount of information that is put into the brain and runs riot there, undigested all your life. We must have life- building, man-making, character making, assimilation of ideas." Education should unveil the divinity is man and this divinity should be seen in treating lunatics, in punishing criminals and in everything that is connected with human life.

In any case it is the thought force of a nation that determines the character of its people. He says, "Thoughts live; they far And so take care of what you think."[3]

Vivekananda suggests that education should lay proper emphasis on creativity, originality and excellence. To him good education is only that which unfolds all the hidden powers in man. Real education requires the cultivations of a sense of humility. This sense of humility is the basis of man's character, the true mark of a balanced personality.

The character of any man is really the aggregate of his innate tendencies, the sum total of the bent of mind. Both pleasure and pain, misery and happiness, are equal factors in the formation of his character. In studying the characters of great men the world has produced, it would be found that it was misery that taught more than happiness.

What India wants is character and strengthening of the will. The will is Almighty and if one continue to exercise his will, he is sure to go higher and higher. It is strength of will or character that can cleave through wells of difficulties. "Watch a man his most common actins; those are indeed the things which will tell you the character of a great man."[4]

Karma and Character

There are two tendencies in human nature; one to harmonise the ideal with life and the other to elevate the life to the ideal. The Karma or action of a person determines the quality of his education. To Swamiji, all the actions in the world and all the movements in human society are simply the manifestation of the will of man. All the scientific discoveries are also manifestations of the will of man. All the scientific discoveries are also manifestations of the will of man : and this 'will' is caused by character and character is manufactured by 'Karma'. As is 'Karma', so is the manifestation of the will.

"Karma in its effect on character is the most tremendous power that man has to deal with."

The Ideal Man

The ideal of every educated man should be perfect unselfishness. When a man has no more self in him, no possession, nothing to call 'me' or 'mine', he becomes an ideal man. It is only through renunciation that somebody can attain that goal. An ordinary human being cannot reach that state of mind; yet he can worship that ideal and slowly struggle to reach it. "True civilization should mean the power of taking the animal-man out of his sense-life, by giving him visions and tasks of planes much higher and not external comforts."

No great work can be without sacrifice. The kind of work for a motive brings misery. That work alone brings nonattachment and bliss, wherein man works as a master of his own mind. So a man who masters his mind is the ideal man, the really educated man.

Leadership Qualities

A good system of education never fails to promote leadership qualities in the growing generation. The leader is to be made aware of the fact that he is a servant of servants and must accommodate a thousand minds. The success of his undertakings depends wholly upon his attitude towards his brethren. He must bear with every one's shortcomings. A leader must be impersonal in his love. In the western world, along with the spirit of independence the spirit of obedience is equally is equally strong. But in India every one is self-important, and that attitude never produces any work. In doing great works, the commands of the leader have to be implicitly obeyed.

In cultivating the virtue of obedience one need not sacrifice one's faith. In any organisation the leader should be of an ideal character. "There is no allegiance possible where there is no character in the leader, and perfect purity ensures the most lasting allegiance and confidence."

Devotion to Duty

The great messengers and prophets have always stressed the importance of devotion to duty. To Vivekananda, duty is sweet only through love and love shines in freedom alone. To the educated mind, all duties are good because there is no expectation for reward.

The Gita suggests that every work must necessarily be a mixture of good and evil. Good and evil will both have their results but the doer must be interested only in action. "He who in good action sees that there is something evil in it, and in the midst of evil that there is something good in it somewhere, has known the secret of work."

Non-Interference

The Principle of non-interference it clear that there are gradations of duty and of morality, that the duty of one state of life, in one set of circumstances will not and cannot be that of another. Education should help every man to take up his own ideal and endeavour to accomplish it. That is a surer way of progress than taking up another man's ideals, which he can never hope to accomplish. " All of men and women in any society are not of the same mind, capacity or of the same power to do things; they must have different ideals and we have no right to sneer at an ideal."

Work Like a Master

The Vedanta teaches men to have faith in themselves first. The best gifts that education can give a man is to make him work like a master and not a slave. If one can take the position of a giver and finds happiness in it, then his work can be taken as worship. Education must impart the spirit of self confidence in dealing with human problems. To Vivekananda the real personality of man, the real love of man that makes him work as a master for the pleasure of work. Swamiji's cherished desire was that to accomplish his duties, "one should be pure, simple and sincere to the backbone." Every educated man must have behind him tremendous integrity, tremendous sincerity and that is the cause of his success in life. He may not have been perfectly selfish ; yet he was tending towards it.

Patriotism and Freedom

Vivekananda believes that education must provide three things for the development of patriotism and freedom. They are: (1) love for the mother country, (2) a strong will to desist evil, and (3) stead – fastness in achieving the desired goal. His deep convictions about patriotism and freedom are very vividly seen in many of his poems and particularly in the third stanza of the 'Song of the Sanyasin."

"Strike off thy fetters! Bonds that bind thee down,

Of shining gold, or darker, baser ore,

Love hat – good, bad – and all the dual thorny,

Know, slave is slave, caressed or whipped, not free;

For fetters, through of gold, are not less strong to bind;

Then off with them, sannyasin bold! say—

"Om Tat sat, Om."[5]

These lines clearly brings out the socio-political and cultural degradation of India in the 19th century and how Vivekananda prepared the people of India to fight for their freedom and independence.

Education of the Masses

The order of the world today is said to be guide and controlled by majority opinion. But the tyranny of the minority over the majority is the most dreadful of all evils. A few men who are at the helm of affairs cannot make a nation move and it is only through education that the whole population can participate in nation building activities.

Most of the reforms that were introduced in the past had been ornamental. These reforms were meant only for the first two castes and not for the lower ones. Education alone can reform the poor, the ill-clothed and the half-starved. "Put the fire there and let it burn upwards and make the Indian nation."

In this age of ránk materialism no one understands his own real nature; every one is for pleasure, pomp and glory and there is no love for the distressed or the downtrodden. The West is groaning under the tyranny of the moneylenders and the East is groaning under the tyranny of the Priests; each must keep the other in check. Vivekananda always said "No priest-craft, no social tyranny—more bread, more opportunity for everybody."

The west requires more spiritual realisation and the east more material. The only service to be done for the lower classes in India is to give them education, to develop their lost individuality. Priestcraft and foreign conquests have trodden them down for centuries. They are to be given ideas, their eyes are to be opened so that they may see what is going on in the world around them.

The great need of India today, he said is "missionaries should educate the people industrially, socially and not religiously" because the people have enough religion in them. In his opinion, no amount of politics would be of any avail until the masses in India are well-educated, well-fed and well-cared for. "They pay for our education, they build our temples, but in turn, they get kicks." In one of his letters to Alasingh in 1894, he expresses his deep concern for the poor. He writes: "My heart is too full to express my feeling; you know it, you can imagine it. So long as the millions live in hunger and ignorance, I hold every man a traitor, who having been educated at their expense, pays the least heed to them."

The Vivekananda, the masses in India are like the sleeping Leviathan. The education imparted by the present university system reaches only a few privileged people. And even those who get that, do not succeed in their endeavours of doing any good to their country. Let the message be spread that they should no longer sleep. The country should awake and live up to its ideals. "Arise, Awake and Sleep not till the goal is reached." It is easy to instruct the masses in simple words in their mother-tongue about the necessities of life, about trade, commerce and things like that which may attract their attention.

In his opinion, India should take the Japanese model for her material progress. Japan became highly industrialised by its hard labour. India lulls with her past glories; it does no work, and hence all the difficulties.

Vivekananda believe that the poor people are the backbone of the nation. If they stop work, there will be no food, no clothing, nothing of that kind. Engrossed in the struggle for existence they do not get the opportunity for awakening of knowledge. They have been working hard all these years uniformly like machines guided by human intelligence. The clever educated sections have taken the substantial part of the fruits of their labour. In every country this has been the case.

Now the masses of Europe and America have been awakened. Signs of this awakening have shown themselves in India, as is evident from the number of strikes among lower classes nowadays. Therefore, the primary task of education is to spread education among the masses. Vivekananda says, "Tell them and make them understand that they are brothers and sisters so that they may be roused by the language of love.... Kindle their knowledge with the help of modern science. Teach them history, geography, science, literature and along with these the profound truths of religion. "With the attainment of knowledge the porter can do his work in a better way, a peasant can be a better peasant. The upper classes should feel this need. They should go to the doors of the poor carrying the great message of fearlessness. It is a curse that laziness, meanness and hypocrisy have covered the whole of India and yet the privileged sections believe that they are educated. Swamiji expresses his scorn about the so called educated men, when he says "Getting by heart the thoughts of others in a foreign language and stuffing their brains with them and taking some university degrees, you consider yourself educated."

Vivekananda has nothing but contempt towards 'Don't touchism' and other social evils of India. He opines "Don't touchism is a form of mental disease. Beware! All expansion is life, all contraction is death." Men of attainment and vision may form groups and make a caste of their own. But the degenerated caste system on the basis of birth should be rooted out from India at any price.

Vivekananda wants every man of the 'Sattva' nature to rise up and be a Brahmin. Those who attain Brahmana-hood must work hard to raise the Indian people by teaching them what they know, by giving out the culture that have accumulated. The non-Brahmanas on the other hand, must be prepared to listen to them and educate themselves for acquiring the true Brahmana culture. To him, "The only way to brings about the levelling of castes is to appropriate the culture, the education which is the strength of the higher castes."

Emancipation of Women

Through the Vedanta declares that both men and women have the same self in them is much difference in India between them then anywhere in the world. In the vedic and upanishadic age, women enjoyed almost every privilege as men but latter the priests had deprived them of their rights. A country's greatness is usually judged by the way in which it shows respect towards her women. In America men look upon their in light and treat well.

The principal reason why India has degenerated is that there is no respect for women. The women of India have long been trained in helplessness and servile dependence on others. Education alone can solve their many and varied problems. To Vivekananda, "Women must be put in a position to solve their own problems in their own way and Indian women are as capable of doing it as any in the world."

India requires great and fearless women to continue the tradition of Ahalya Bai and Mira Bai—women fit to be mothers of heroes bound by the principles of chastity and purity.

Education of women should be spread with religion as its centre. It may go a long way in the formation of character and observance of celebacy.

The ideal of a perfect women is to be found in Sita, in the great epic Ramayana, and every Indian women should try to attain that greatness and strength. In the vedic or upanishadic ages also there were similar examples like Maitreyi and Gargi who had taken the place of rishis through their wonderful eruditions in philosophy. The first thing. That is required, is to intensify this ideal of women hood in the Indian women so that they may feet the necessity of coming up along with men. Along with that they should be taught the sciences and other things which would be of real use to them.

Considering the needs of his age, Vivekananda feels it imperative to train some women in the ideals of renunciation in order that they may work as Brahmacharinis for women's welfare and progress. In his opinion society in every country shapes its destiny. "So we need not trouble our heads about such reforms as the abolition of early marriage or the remarriage of widows." The main task of Indian is to impart education to both men and women alike. As an out come of that education, they will be able to decide what is good for them. In the education of women can be included subjects like Religion, Arts, Science, Home management, Cooking, Sewing and Hygiene. For this trained Brahmacharinis should go to the villages and towns, open centres, and do hard work. Along with other things, Japa, worship and meditation shall form an indispensable part of teaching.

Vivekananda hopes that the women who get themselves trained in these centres will make further progress in the virtues that distinguish them form the rest. The children of such mothers will prove themselves to be worthy citizens of India". "It is only in the hands of educated and pious mothers that great men are born." The ideal women in India is the mother, the mother first and the mother last. From this mother hood comes tremendous responsibility on women. The mother is the ideal of love. She rules the family, she possesses the family, "To the ordinary man in India, the whole force of womanhood is concentrated in motherhood."

No women should any longer remain content in an inferior position. In most of the western countries women have gained considerable importance in their race for equated with men. But blind imitation of the West cannot be equated with the social progress of India. In the West the spiritual aims of human life are not uppermost as it in India. It is spiritual ideal of Sita that Indian women have been following through the ages. Faith in God, self abnegation and service have marked their character, and chastity has the guiding motive of their life.

REFERENCES

1. Swami Nirvedanand, *Swami Vivekananda on India and He Problem*, Almora Advait Ashrma, 1971. p. 41.
2. C.W. Vol. III, 1973, p. 160.
3. T.S. Avinashlingam, Education Coimbtore, Ramkrishna Mission, 1967, p. 47.
4. Swami Ranganathanand, Swami Vivekananda on Universal Ethics and Moral conduct, Ramkrishna Math, 1974, p. 37. This point is well maintained by Mahatma Gandhi, who used to say: "The character of a person is not revealed through big achievement but through small bits of actions performed by him."
5. C.W. Vol. IV, 1972, p. 393.

6

Aims of Education

Education for Character According to Vivekananda

The character of any man is but the aggregate of his tendencies, the sum total of the bent of his mind. As pleasure and pain pass before his soul, they leave upon it different pictures, and the result of these combined impressions is what is called a man's character.[1] We are what our thoughts have made us.[2] Each thought is a little hammer blow on the lumps of iron which our bodies are, manufacturing out of it what we want it to be.[3] Words are secondary. Thoughts live; they travel far. And so take care of what you think. Good and evil have an equal share in moulding character and in some cases misery is a greater teacher than happiness. In studying the great characters the world has produced, I daresay, in the vast majority of cases, it would be found that it was misery that taught more than happiness, it was poverty that taught more than wealth, and it was blows that brought out their inner fire more than praise.[4] Brought up in lap of luxury, lying on a bed of roses and never shedding a tear, who has become great? When there comes affection in the heart, when the storm of sorrow blows all round, and it seems as if light will be seen no more, when hope and courage are almost gone, it is then, in the midst of this spiritual tempest, that the light within gleams.[5]

Using the simile of a lake for the mind, every ripple, every wave that rises in the mind, when it subsides, does not die out entirely, but leaves a mark and future possibility of that mark coming out again....Every work that we do, every movement of the body, every thought that we think, leaves such an impression on the mind stuff, and even when such impressions are not obvious on the surface, they are sufficiently strong to work beneath the surface, subconsciously. What we are every moment is determined by the sum total of these impressions on the mind.... Each man's character is determined by the sum total of these impressions. If good impressions prevail, the character becomes good, if bad, it becomes bad. If a man continuously hears bad words, thinks bad thoughts, does bad actions, his mind will be full of bad impressions, and they will influence his thought and work without his being conscious of the fact. In fact, these bad impressions are always working. The sum total of these impressions in him will create the strong motive power for doing bad actions. He will be like a machine in the hands of his impressions.

Similarly if a man thinks good thoughts and does good work, the sum total of these impressions will be good and they in a similar manner will force him to do good in spite of himself. When a man has done so much good work and thought so many good thoughts, there is an irresistible tendency in him to do good. Even if he wishes to do evil, his mind as the sum total of his tendencies, will not allow him to do so. He is completely under the influence of the good tendencies. When such is the case, a man's good character is said to be established.[6] If you really want to judge the character of a man, look not at his great performances. Watch a man do his most common actions; those are indeed the things which will tell you the real character of the great man. Great occasions rouse even the lowest of human beings to some kind of greatness, but he alone is really great whose character is great always—the same wherever he be.[7]

When a large number of these impressions is left on the mind, they coalesce and become a habit. It is said, 'Habit is second nature.' It is first nature also and the whole nature of man. Everything that we are is the result of habit.... That gives us consolation because, if it is only habit, we can make it and unmake it at any time. The only remedy for bad habits is counter habits is counter habits . All the bad habits can be controlled by good habits. Go on doing good, thinking holy thoughts continuously. That is the only way to suppress base impressions. Never say any man is hopeless, because he only represents a character, a bundle of habits, which can be checked by new and better ones. Character is repeated habits and repeated habits and repeated habits alone can reform character.[8]

The cause of all apparent evil is in ourselves. Do not blame any supernatural being. Neither be hopeless or despondent, nor think that we are in a place from which we can never escape unless someone comes and gives a helping hand. We are like silkworms. We make the thread of our own substance and spin the cocoon, and in course of time are imprisoned inside. The network of *karma* we have woven around ourselves. And in our ignorance we feel as if we are bound, and weep and wail for help. But help does not come from without; it comes from within ourselves. Cry to all the gods of the universe. I cried for years and in the end I found that I was helped. But help came with in. And I had to unto what I had done by mistake. I had to cut the net which I had thrown round myself. I have committed many mistakes in my life. But mark you, without those mistakes, I should not be what I am today. I do not mean that you are to go home and wilfully commit mistakes; do not misunderstand me in that way. But do not mope because of mistake you have committed.[9]

We commit mistakes because we are weak, and we are weak because we are ignorant. Who makes us ignorant? We ourselves. We put our hands our, eyes and weep that it is dark. Take the hands away and there is light. The light exists always for us, the self-effulgent nature of the human soul. Do you not hear what modern scientific men say? What is the cause of evolution? Desire. The animal wants to do something but does not find the environment favourable, and therefore develops a new body. Who develops it? The animal itself: its will. Continue to exercise your will and it will take you higher. The will is almighty. If it is almighty, you say: why cannot I do everything?

But you are thinking only of your little self. Look back on yourself from the state of the amoeba to the human being; who made all that? Your own will. Can you deny that it is almighty? That which has made you come up so high, can make you go higher still. What you want is character, strengthening of the will.[10]

If you go home sit in sack cloth and ashes, and weep your lives out because you took certain false steps, it will not help you but will weaken you all the not help you, but will weaken you all the more. If this room is full of darkness for thousands of years and you come in and begin to weep and wail, will the darkness vanish? Strike a match and light comes in a moment. What good will it do to you to think all your lives, 'Oh, I have done evil; I have made many mistakes.'? It requires no ghost to tell us that. Bring in the light and evil goes in a moment. Build up your character and manifest your real nature, the Effulgent, the Resplendent, the Ever- Pure and call it up in every one see.[11]

Development of Personality

You see what is happening all around us. The world is one of influence. Part of our energy is used up in the preservation of our own bodies. Beyond that, every particle of our energy is day and night being used in influencing others. Our bodies, our virtues, our intellect, and our spirituality, all these are continuously influencing others; and so, conversely, we are being influenced by them. This is going on all around us. Now, to take concrete example: a man comes, you know he is very learned, his language is beautiful and he speaks to you by the hour—but he does not make any impression. Another man comes, and he speaks a few words, not well arranged ungrammatical perhaps; all the same , he makes an immense impression. Many of you have seen that. So it is evident that words alone cannot always produce an impression. Words, even thoughts, contribute only one-third of the influence in making an impression, the man, two thirds. What you call the personal magnetism of the man—that is what is what goes out and impresses you.

Coming to great leaders of mankind, we always find that it was the personality of the man that counted. Now, take all the great authors of the past, the great thinkers. Really speaking. How many thoughts have they thought? Takes all the writings that have been left to us by the past leaders of mankind; take each one of their books and appraise them. The real thoughts, new and genuine, that have been thought in this world up to this time, amount to only a handful. Read in their books the thoughts they have left to us. The authors do not appear to be giants to us, and yet we know that they were great giants in their days. What made them so ? Not simply the thoughts they thought, neither the books they wrote, nor the speeches they made, it was something else that is now gone, that is their personality. As I have already remarked, the personality of the man is two thirds, and his intellect, his words are but one-third. It is the real man, the personality of the man, that runs through us. Our actions are but effects. Actions must come when the man is there; the effect is bound to follow the cause.

The ideal of all education, all training, should be this man-making. But, instead of that, we are always trying to polish up the outside. What use polishing up the outside when there is no inside? The end aim of all training is to make the grow. The man who influences, who throws his magic, as it were, upon his fellow-beings, is a dynamo of power, and when that man is ready, he can do anything he likes: that personality put upon anything will make it work.

Now we see that though this is a fact, no physical laws that we know of will explain this. How can we explain it by chemical and physical knowledge? How much of oxygen, hydrogen, carbon—how many molecules in different positions, and how many cells, etc., etc., can explain this mysterious personality? And we still see, it is a fact, and not only that, it is the real man; and it is that man that lives and moves and works, it is that man that influences, moves his fellow-being and passes out, and his intellect and books and works are but traces left behind. Think of this. Compare the great teachers of religion with the great philosophers. The philosophers scarcely influenced anybody's inner man, and yet they wrote most marvellous books. The religious teachers, on the other hand, moved countries in their lifetime. The difference was made by personality. In the philosopher it is a faint personality that influences; in the great Prophets it is tremendous. In the former we touch the intellect, in the latter we touch life. In the one case, it is simply a chemical process, putting certain chemical ingredients together which may gradually combine and under proper circumstances brings out a flash of light or may fail. In the other, it is like a torch that goes round quickly, lighting others.

The science of Yoga claims that it has discovered the laws which develop this personality, and by proper attention to those laws and methods, each one can grow and strengthen his personality. This is one of the great practical things and this is the secret of all education. This has a universal application. In the life of the house-holder, in the life of the poor, the rich the man of the business, the spiritual man, in every one's life, it is a great thing, the strengthening of this personality. They are laws, very fine, which are behind the physical laws, as know. That is to say, there are no such realities as a physical world, a mental world, a spiritual word. Whatever is, is one. Let us say, it is a sort of tapering existence, the thickest part is here, it tapers and becomes finer; the finest is what we call Spirit; the grossest, the body. And just as it is here, in the microcosm, it is exactly the same in the macrocosm. This universe of ours is exactly like that; it is the gross external thickness, and it tapers in to something finer and finer until it become God.

We also know that the greatest power is lodged in the fine, not in the coarse. We see a man take up a huge weight, we see his muscles swell, and all over his body we signs of exertion, and we think the muscles are powerful things. But it is the thin thread-like things, the nerves, which bring power to the muscles; the moment one of these threads is cut off from reaching the muscles, they are not able to work at all. These tiny nerves bring the power from something finer still—thought, and so on. So it is the fine that is really the seat of power. Of course we can see the movements in the gross; but when fine movements take place, we cannot see them. When a gross thing moves, we catch it, and thus we naturally identify movement with things which are gross. But all the power is really in the fine. We do not see any movement in the fine, perhaps because the movement is so intense that we cannot perceive it. But if by any science, any investigation, we are helped to get hold of these finer forces which are the cause of the expression, the expression itself will be under control. There is a little bubble coming from the bottom of a lake; we do not see it coming all the time, we see it only when it bursts on the surface; so, we can perceive thoughts only after they develop a great deal, or after they become actions. We constantly complain that we have no control over our actions, over our thoughts. But how can we have it? If we can get control over the fine movements, if we can get hold of thought at the root, before it has become thought, before it has become action, then it would be possible for us to control the whole. Now, if there is a method by which we can analyse, investigate, understand and finally grapple with those finer powers, the finer causes, then alone is it possible to have control over ourselves, and the man who has control over his own mind assuredly will have control over every other mind. That is why purity and morality have been always the object of religion; a pure moral man has control of himself. And all minds are the same, different parts of one Mind. He who knows one lump of clay has known all day in universe. He who knows and controls his own mind knows the secret of every mind and has power over every mind.

Each man in his childhood runs through the stages through which his race has come up; only the race took thousands of years to do it, while the child takes a few years. The child is first the old savage man-and he crushes a butterfly under his feet. The child is at first like the primitive ancestors of his race. As he grows, he passes through different stages until he reaches the development of his race. Only he does it swiftly and quickly. Now, take the whole of humanity as a race, or take the whole of the animal creation, man and the lower animals, as one whole. There is an end towards which the whole is moving. Let us call it perfection. Some men and women are born who anticipate the whole progress of mankind. In stead of waiting and being reborn over and again for ages until the whole human race has attained to that perfection, they, as it were , rush through them in a few short years of their life. And we know that we can hasten these processes, if we be true to ourselves. If a number of men without any culture, be left to live upon an island, and are given barely enough food, clothing and shelter, they will gradually go on and on, evolving higher and higher stages of civilisation. We know also, that this growth can be hastened by additional means. We help the growth of trees, do we not? Left to nature they would have grown, only they would have taken a longer time; we help them to grow in a shorter time than they would otherwise have taken. We are doing all the time the some thing, hastening the growth of things by artificial means . Why cannot we hasten the growth of man? We can do that as a race. Why are teachers sent to other countries? Because by these means we can hasten the growth of races. Now, can we not hasten the growth of individuals? We can. Can we put a limit to the hastening? We cannot say how much a man can grow in one life. You have no reason to say that this much can do and no more. Circumstances can hasten him wonderfully. Can there be any limit then, till you come to perfection? So, what comes of it? That a perfect man, that is to say the type that is to come of this race, perhaps millions of years hence, that man, can come today.

All great Incarnations and Prophets are such men; they reached perfection in this one life. We have had such men at all periods of the world's history and at all times. Quite recently there was such a man who lived the life of the whole human race and reached the end—even in this life. Even this hastening of the growth must be under laws. Suppose we can investigate these laws and understand their secrets and apply them to our own needs; it follows that we grow. We hasten our growth, we hasten our development, and we become perfect, even in this life. This is the higher part of our life, and the science of the study of mind and its powers has this perfection as its real end.

The utility of this science is to bring out the perfect man, and not let him wait and wait for ages, just a plaything in the hands of the physical world, like a log of drift-wood carried from wave to wave and tossing about in the ocean. This science wants you to be strong, to take the work in your own hand, instead of leaving it in the hands of nature, and get beyond this little life.[12]

REFERENCES

1. C.W. Vol. I, p. 27.
2. C.W. Vol. VII, p. 14.
3. C.W. Vol. VII, p. 20.
4. C.W. Vol. I, p. 27.
5. C.W. Vol. IV, p. 492.
6. C.W. Vol. I, p. 54.
7. C.W. Vol. I, p. 29.
8. *Ibid.*, Vol. I, p. 208.
9. *Ibid.*, Vol. II, pp. 355-6.
10. *Ibid.*, Vol. II, pp. 356-7.
11. *Ibid.*, Vol. II, p. 357.
12. *Ibid.*, Vol. I, pp. 13-19.

7

The Teacher Taught Relationship

Vivekananda says: My idea of education is *Gurugrha-vasa*. Without the personal life of the teacher, there would be no education.[1] One should live from his very boyhood with one whose character is a blazing fire and should have before him a living example of the highest teaching. In our country the imparting of knowledge has always been through men of renunciation. The charge of imparting knowledge should again fall upon the shoulders of Tyagis. [2]

The old system of education in India was very different from the modern system. The students had not to pay. It was thought that knowledge is so sacred that no man ought to sell it. Knowledge should be given freely and without any price. The teachers used to take students without charge and not only so, most of them gave their students food and clothes. The support these teachers, the wealthy families made gifts to them and they in their turn had to maintain their students. [3] The disciple of old used to repair to the hermitage of the Guru, fuel in hand, and the Guru, after ascertaining his competence, would teach him the Vedas, fastening round his waist the threefold filament of Munja, a kind of grass, as the emblem of his vow to keep his body, mind and speech in control.[4]

There are certain conditions necessary in the taught and also in the teacher.[5] The conditions necessary for the taught are purity, a real thirst after knowledge, and perseverance. Purity in thought, speech and act is absolutely necessary. As for thirst after knowledge, it is an old law that we all get whatever we want. None of us can get anything other than what we fix our hearts upon. There must be a continuous struggle, a constant fight, an unremitting grappling with our lower nature, till the higher want is actually felt and victory is achieved. The student who sets out with such a spirit of perseverance will surely find success at last.[6]

In regard to the teacher, we must see that he knows the spirit of the scriptures. The whole world reads Bibles, Vedas and Korans; but they are all only words, syntax, etymology, philology—the dry bones of religion. The teacher who deals too much in words and allows the mind to be carried away by the force of word loses the spirit. It is the knowledge of the spirit of the scriptures alone that constitutes the true teacher. The second condition necessary for the teacher is sinlessness. The question is often asked: 'Why should we look into the character and personality of teacher?' This is not right. The *sine qua non* of acquiring truth for oneself, or for imparting to others, is purity of heart and soul. He must be perfectly pure and then only comes the value of his words.[7] The function of the teacher is indeed an affair of the transference of something and not one of mere stimulation of existing intellectual or other faculties in the taught. Something real and appreciable as an influence comes from the teacher and goes to the taught. Therefore, the teacher must be pure. The third condition is in regard to the motive. The teacher must not teach with any ulterior selfish motive, for money, name or fame. His work must be simply out of love, out of pure love for mankind at large. The only medium through which spiritual force can be transmitted is love. Any selfish motive, such as the desire for gain or name, will immediately destroy the conveying medium.[8]

It is not easy to be a disciple. The first condition is that the student who wants to know the truth must give up all desires for gain. What we see is not truth as long as any desire creeps into our minds. So long as there is in the heart the least desire for the world, truth will not come. The rich understand truth much less than the poor people. The rich man has no time to think of anything beyond his wealth and power, his comforts and indulgences. I do not trust the man who never weeps; he has a big block of granite where his heart should be. Therefore knowing what prosperity means and what happiness means, one should give up these and seek to know the truth and truth alone. Unselfishness is more paying, only people have not the patience to practise it. It is more paying from the point of view of health also. Love, truth and unselfishness are not merely moral figures of speech, but they form our highest ideal, because in them lies such a manifestation of power. Self-restraint is a manifestation of greater power than all outgoing action. All outgoing energy following a selfish motive is frittered away; it will not cause power to return to you; but if restrained, it will result in development of power. This self-control will tend to produce a mighty will, a character which makes a Christ or a Buddha.

The second condition is that a disciple must be able to control the internal and external senses. By hard practice he has to arrive at the stage where he can assert his mind against the commands of nature. He should be able to say to his mind, 'You are mine; I order you, do not see or hear anything.' Next the mind must be made to quiet down. It is rushing about. Just as I sit down to mediate, all the vilest subjects in the world come up. The whole thing is nauseating. Why should the mind think thoughts I do not want it to think? I am as it were a slave to the mind. No spiritual knowledge is possible so long as the mind is restless and out of control. The disciple has to learn to control the mind.

Also, the disciple must have great power of endurance. Life seems comfortable, and you find the mind behaves well when everything is going well with you. But if something goes wrong, your mind loses its balance. That is not good. Bear all evil and misery without one murmur or hurt, without one thought of unhappiness, resistance, remedy or retaliation. That is true endurance. When my Master, Sri Ramakrishna fell ill, a Brahmin suggested to him that he apply his tremendous mental power to cure himself; he said that if my Master would only concentrate his mind on the diseased part of the body, it would heal. Sri Ramakrishna answered, "What! Bring down the mind that I've given to God to this little body!" He refused to think of body and illness. His mind was continually conscious of God; it was dedicated to Him utterly. He would not use it for any other purpose. Remember also the man on the Gross! He pitied those who crucified him. He endured every humiliation and suffering. He took the burden of all upon himself: "Come unto me, all yet that labour and are heavy laden, and I will give you rest." Such is true endurance. How very high he was above this life, so high that we cannot understand it!

The next condition the disciple must fulfil is to conceive an extreme desire to be free. No one is desiring anything beyond the body. What is the world but a combination of stomach and sex? Look at millions of men and women—that is what they are living for. Take these away from them and they will find their life empty, meaningless and intolerable. Such are we. And such is our mind; it is continually hankering for ways and means to satisfy the hunger for the stomach and sex. These desires of the body bring only momentary satisfaction and endless suffering. It is like drinking a cup of which the surface layer is nectar, while underneath all is a poison. But we still hanker for all these things. Renunciation of the senses and desires is the only way out of this misery. If you want to be spiritual, you must renounce. This is the real test. Give up the world—this nonsense of the senses. There is only one real desire; to know what is true, to be spiritual. No more materialism, no more this egoism. I must become spiritual. Strong, intense must be the desire. If a man's hands and feet were so tied that he could not move and then if a burning piece of charcoal were placed on his body, he would struggle with all his power to throw it off. When I shall have that sort of extreme desire, that restless struggle to throw off this burning world, then the time will have come for me to glimpse the Divine truth.

Our sole concern should be to know the highest truth. Our goal is the loftiest. Let us worship the spirit in spirit, standing on spirit. Let the foundation be spirit; the middle, spirit; the culmination, spirit. Stand thou in the spirit! That is the goal. We know we cannot reach it yet. Never mind. Do not despair, but do not drag the ideal down. The important thing is: how much less you think of the body, of yourself as matter, as dead, dull, insentient matter, how much more you think of yourself as shining immortal being. The more you think of yourself as shining immortal spirit, the more eager you will be to be absolutely free of matter, body and senses. This is the intense desire to be free.

There are the conditions which a man who wants to be a disciple must fulfil; without fulfilling them he will not be able to come in contact with the true Guru. And even if he is fortunate enough to find him, he will not be quickened by the power that the Guru may transmit. There cannot be any compromising of these conditions. With the fulfillment of these conditions the lotus of the disciple's heart will open and the bee shall come. Then the disciple knows that the Guru was within himself. He opens out. He realises. He crosses the ocean of life, goes beyond, and in mercy, without a thought of gain or praise, he in his turn helps others to cross.[9]

With the teacher our relationship is the same as that between ancestor and his descendant. Without faith, humility, submission and veneration in our hearts towards the teacher, there cannot be any growth in us. In those countries which have neglected to keep up this kind of relation, the teacher has become a mere lecturer, the teacher expecting his five dollars and the person taught expecting his brain to be filled with the teacher's words and each going his own way after this much is done.[10] But too much faith in personality has a tendency to produce weakness and idolatry. Worship your Guru as God, but do not obey him blindly. Love him all you will, but think for yourself.[11]

The teacher must throw his whole force into the tendency of the taught. Without real sympathy we can never teach well.[12] Do not try to disturb the faith of any man. If you can, give him something better, but do not destroy what he has. The only true teacher is he who can convert himself, as it were, into a thousand persons at a moment's notice. The true teacher is he who can immediately come down to the level of the student, and transfer his soul to the student's soul and see through and understand through his mind. Such a teacher can really teach and none else.[13]

REFERENCES

1. Complete works of Swami Vivekananda, Vol. V, p. 224.
2. *Ibid.*, Vol. V, p. 369.
3. *Ibid.*, Vol. IV, pp. 162-3.
4. *Ibid.*, Vol. VI, p. 472.
5. *Ibid.*, Vol. IV, p. 24.
6. *Ibid.*, Vol. III, pp. 48-9.
7. *Ibid.*, Vol. III, p. 50.
8. *Ibid.*, Vol. III, p. 51.
9. *Ibid.*, Vol. VIII, pp. 107-121.
10. *Ibid.*, Vol. III, p. 52.
11. *Ibid.*, Vol. VII, p. 85-86.
12. *Ibid.*, Vol. VII, p. 99.
13. *Ibid.*, Vol. IV, p. 183.

8

Education for Cultural and Global Values

Cultural components play very important role in any system of education. They are of national importance. Martin Luther (1483 – 1546) has rightly observed in this regard, "The personality of the country depends not on the bun dance of its revenues, not on the strength of its fortifications, nor on the beauty of its public-buildings but its cultivated citizens, in its men of education, enlightenment and character.

It is the quality of country men, which decides the class or quality of a nation. Our Cherished aim has been spiritualism and not materialism. The spiritual values have been main pointers or indicators of the quality of the persons in India. Education is one of the patent tools for these values. In the words of K.G. Saiyidain, "It is a matter of making better men and women, compared to which everything is secondary – machines, factories, buildings, dams, pictures, music and systems of thought. It is maintenance and enrichment of culture. It is the preservation and reconstruction of values, not social and cultural agencies. It is sharing audicioussly in God's creativity."

India's cultural heritage is so varied, and so enriched that it is capable of meeting and any challenge. The present value-crisis is originated mainly due to mis-conceptualization of modernity and cut-throat competition for acquisition of more and more material wealth, which is uniquely intensified due to rapid growth of Science and technology.

In the modern perspective main tenets of the New culture can be enumerated as following:

1. We accept life with all its joys and sorrows. We shall make no effort to transcend it.
2. The goal of living is to make the life good, happy and beautiful for oneself and for other human beings.
3. If we believe that we are to be born again and again in this world, we should see to it that every time we are born, we find the world better.
4. The goal of life will be achieved through the individual that acquiring maturity an moral integrity through the society founded on the principles of equality and social interest and through the state creating conditions fit for achieving the goal.[1]

Swami Vivekananda was a great social reformer with a nationalistic out-look and a humane approach to religion and culture. He was an awakened spirit of India who could interpret various intricacies of religion in the socio-political perspectives prevailing in his time. He had gone deep into the social and political decline of India during his time and attempted to prescribe a workable formula to eradicate all social inequalities. His concept of universalism was Later upheld be Rabindranath Tagore and Mahatma Gandhi. He was one of the prominent cultural revivalists and as such he laid more stress on cultural components in education. His address to the audience as 'my brother and sisters' is a classical testimony of his 'universalism'.

National Plan of Education

Education on national lines has been recognised by all advanced countries as a necessary equipment of national progress. But the system of education in India is yet to realise this great need where millions live without any education at all. To Vivekananda, no education can be called 'national' unless it inspires and ensures love for the mother country. The Indian system is defective in this context and it lacks a comprehensive ideal. There is very little creativity or originality in the education process. There is large scale exploitation in education institutions. The cultural heritage of India is totally ignored. The courses offered in schools and colleges are essentially western courses not suitable to Indian conditions. They are rigidly mechanical which establish no relations. They are rigidly mechanical which establish no relationship between the teacher and the taught. Education on national lines alone can solve these problems. Vivekananda says: "We must have the whole education of our country, spiritual or secular, in our own hands and it must be on national lines through national methods as for as practical."[2]

Education for Culture

worthless if it does not promote a love for the nation. Education as a cultural instrument has a threefold function; conservation, transmission and renewal of culture. Renewal of culture is as much important as conservation and transmission if society is to be dynamic and strong.

To attain this end, the people are to be properly equipped and allowed to compare, contrast, reject or accept the things that are placed before them. No one can expect to strengthen democracy in India merely borrowing the arguments of western thinkers. But it is possible to take up some basic democratic ideas and synthesise them with the nation's cultural heritage.

To Vivekananda the task of the educationlist is to show the people all the ways of economic well-being and leave them to a natural process of self adjustment. For economic and cultural education a well-directed and systematic training of the head, heart and hand is essential. It is on the strength and integration of these faculties that the well-being of the individual and the society depend. Dr. Radhakrishnan remarks "A man's culture is not to be judged by the amount of tabulated information which he has at his command, but the quality of mind which he brings to bear on the facts of life.[3]

Education for Character

To Swami Vivekananda , without humility and character there is no education. Character is nothing but a bundle of habits. When a desire, thought or act is constantly repeated, it becomes a habit. Right thought and right action will lead to right habit and these habits will serve as character traits of a person. What is required for the formation of character is only a change of heart and a change in one's own conception of the world which is actually a projection of one's own mind.

In his opinion, unsophisticated cobler or fisherman who is possessed of character is more education than many who have modern schooling which is nothing but literary training. As Whitehead puts it "Education with inert ideas is not only useless; it is above all things harmful."[4] Vivekananda fully agrees with this view and says that misery of man will continue to exist until man's character-energy is fully utillised for the re-establishment of desirable value of human life.

Masses: The Hope

Vivekananda wanted his followers to go to the sinking millions of India and lift them by hand. In order to order to elucidate this programme he said: "The well-being of the higher classes now lies in helping the lower to get their legitimate right."[5] He thus encouraged the common masses to fight against the upper classes for removing social inequalities. He condemned the upper classes for encouraging priest-craft and social tyranny.

He worked throughout his life for the rights of the poor, the ill-clothed and half-starved by keeping his stronghold on spiritual and secular education. He wanted the nation to introduce nondectarian temples having only "Om" as the symbol, the greatest symbol of any sect. Here should be taught the common grounds of different sects. Facilities may be provide for imparting training to teachers so that they may go about teaching the right meaning of religion and giving secular education to the people at large.

He also suggested that the ideas of the Vedas must be taught in the language of the people; at the same time Sanskrit education must be given because the very sounds of Sanskrit would supply a sense of vitality and strength to the race. In suggesting a correlation between education and national development, Vivekananda felt that the future of India would be in the hands of the common masses. In order to avoid casts distinction he suggested common prayer halls with the symbol of "Om" acceptable to all sections of society.

The Ideal of Womanhood in India

Vivekananda felt that the American women enjoyed more freedom, when compared to that of on Indian women. He considered the women of the west cultured and civilized, free and frank in all their dealings. He denounced the social evils in India, like 'Sati' child marriage, etc., which affected Indian women in several ways. He suggested that the women should be made ambitious through a good system of education. The ideal of womanhood in the East is not only that of Sita or Sarvitri but also that of an ideal mother. "Motherhood is the beginning. Motherhood is the end of India womanhood."[6] In Indian, one can address a girl as "mother following the custom of the land. The Indian women is expected to imitate the life of the mother, which is her first duty. Though this ideal has its own merits, the millions of women in villages are still the victims of ignorance, superstition and disease relying still on age old customs and traditions. So he made a strong appeal for raising the status of women along with that of man. In making a comparison of Indian women with those of the west, he found no reason for their inferior position. He felt that it was much against the ancient ideal of India that women were not given enough opportunities for self-development.

The Curse of Caste System

Vivekananda mercilessly condemned the caste system and untouchability by the Brahmin class. He carefully analysed the causes of social and political evils of the nation and made an earnest effort to eradicate all social inequalities. He was very in his stand on the caste system on the caste system which he said must be abolished at any cost. He did not accept Brahminhood by birth and politics without morals . He said, "The caste is opposed to the religion of the Vedanta."[7] To him the term 'Varna' meant the mental quality of a man and not his physical make up or appearance.

He saw no for anyone to claim superiority over others. His ideas of perfection was extended to all castes and sects. He expected that the lower section would rise to the occasion if they were made conscious of their divinity. The problem of caste system in India is to be tackled by suitable legislation without which no social aim can be achieved.

Vedanta and Science

Vivekananda firmly believes that the vedantic enquiry leads to the unity of consciousness, infinite and non-dual which is the real stuff of the universe. It is termed 'Brahman' or Atman which is beyond the grasp of all terms and concepts. Vedanta holds that the inner nature and the outer nature of man are to be realized as one and that there should be no conflict in his mind. Education, according."[8]

In science, matter is nothing but energy in the wave of function. Similar is the nature of pure consciousness which is beyond the limitations of name, form and action. Vivekananda holds that this 'oneness' is the rationale of all ethics of all ethics and all spiritual it. He considers the Brahmanas God or the Absolute which is equivalent to 'Mahat' or 'Ishwara'. The Mahat or Ishwara is also the primal creative energy which can be apprehended as force and matter. So there is no anti-thesis between God and man, between Vedanta and science.

Awakened India

Vivekananda was a great social reformer whose mind was immanent with the real urge for the resurrection of India's past glory and greatness. Such a resurrection would mean "a process of refinement of the mind which must express itself in tasks and manners." Swamiji had heralded the concept of moral and material well-being of the nation and suggested that all social reforms should be based on cultural and moral strength. He did not welcome drastic and sudden steps. He was against imposing reforms from the top and was very particular that the means should justify the end.

He wanted gradual and peaceful changes through a good system of education and by enlightening the people. He realised that English education had its own contribution to the growth of India's body politic. His emphasis was not on criticising things, but on construction. He always put the stress on the absolute conquest of fear. Being a spiritual monist he was essentially an internationalist. His monumental vedic researches helped him to maintain the highest social and cultural ethics throughout his life.

Today there is a deterioration of cultural ethics and standards. The conflict within castes, groups and nations is a common feature everywhere. The supreme need of the hour is to counteract this emotional, moral and cultural collapse. Only a process of rational education can bring about a healthy political and social life.

Emotional Integration

The problem of emotional integration in India is to be analysed both at the individual and social level. Emotional integration is possible only through social interactions and interpersonal relations. Vivekananda suggested that there should be a sense of identification with the spirit of the nation in all individual and social activities.

In a country like India with a vast population and varied problem, it is essential that increasing socialization should be achieved. Through increasing inter-communication it is possible to suggest a workable programme of emotional integration regardless of parochial and linguistic belongingness. The ideals of universal brotherhood and social justice can be promoted through social accommodation of different of different interests. The scientific ingenuity of man is to be adjusted with his moral insight.

Vivekananda suggests that emotional integration is possible if the different sections of society are reawakened to the need for an inner unity. India's fidelity to the religious roots of emotional integration should be re-established to regain her lost energies. For this, "the society and the educational system should have knowledge of each other."

Education for International Understanding

Though Vivekananda primarily preached the concept of spiritual freedom, his words had always the spell of political freedom and international understanding. His political ideas are found scattered in his lectures from Colombo to Almora, in his comparison between the East and the West and in his discourses on the future of modern India. His inspiring words have influenced mahatma Gandhi and Aurobindo in their political convictions. He always pleaded for human expansion and unity, and taught his countrymen that without the divine remarking of human nature, their civilization would be doomed for ever. "Self-expansion should be the end and aim of true education."

His metaphysics, his philosophy of history and culture and his concept of nationalism actually represented a synthesis of eastern and western cultures. Vivekananda's creed of nationalism, was not narrow and fanatical but was of a cosmopolitan nature. Nationalism was only a necessary stage in the social and political evolution of man. The ultimate aim should be to establish international peace and security by strengthening the spiritual foundations of different nations.

Renunciation and Service

The basic ethical question in the Bhagavat Gita is whether men should renounce actions or whether they should perform them even after the realisation of supreme knowledge.

Vivekananda had mastered all the different yogas and attained Nirvikalpa Samadhi. He would have easily resorted to the life of a Sanyasin in line with the ancient Rishis of India. But he thought that he had a higher mission in the world and hence spent the rest of his life as a Karma-Yogi. Vivekananda pleads that man should perform his duties with a total sense of detachment. The cosmic wheel of existence is a king of divine sacrifice and so every man should do his 'Karma' which means service to humanity. The central point here is to achieve a spiritual awareness of duties and rights to suit the requirements of different situations.

To Vivekananda freedom does not mean licence but the positive power of doing good to others. He wants every man to work day in and day out for the cause of humanity. His ideals of work is the greatest message to the world. He followed the dictum of the Geeta *ad.verbitum* "only duty is they concern and not the fruit."[9]

REFERENCES

1. R.R. Kumaria, What life should mean to an Indian, p. 103
2. Complete works of Swami Vivekananda, Vol. III, 1972, p.302.
3. S. Radhakhishnan, Freedom and Culture, Madras, Natesan, 1936, p.20.
4. A.N. Whitehead, Aims of Education and Other Essays and other Essays, London, Williams and Norgate, 1960, p.2.
5. C.W. Vol. VII, p.149.
6. Maithilyanand Swami, "*The Ideal of Woman hood*", Vedant Kesari, December 1959.
7. C.W. Vol. V, p. 311.
8. T.S. Avinashlingam, Educational Philosophy of Swami Vivekand, Coimbatore, Sh. Ramkrishna Vidyalaya, 1974, p. 19.
9. कर्मण्येवाधिकारस्ते मा फलेषु कदाचन। —Geeta

9 Education of the Masses

Vivekananda Says

My heart aches to think of the condition of the poor, the low in India. They sink lower every day. They feel the blow showered upon them by a cruel society, but they do not know whence the blow comes. They have forgotten that they too are men.[1] My heart is too full to express my feelings. So long as the millions live in hunger and ignorance, I hold every man a traitor who, having been educated at their expense, pays not the least heed to them.[2] Our great national sin is the neglect of the masses and is the cause of our downful. No amount of politics would be of any avail until the masses in India are once more well educed, well-fed and well-cared for.[3]

A nation is advanced in proportion as education and intelligence spread among the masses. The chief cause of India's ruin has been the monopolising of the whole education and intelligence of the land among a handful of men. If we are to rise again, we shall have to do it by spreading education among the masses.[4] The only service to be done for our lower classes is to give them education to develop their individuality. They are to be given ideas. Their eyes are to be opened to what is going on in the world around them, and then will work our their own salvation. Every nation, every man and every woman an must work out their own salvation. Give them ideas that is the only help they require and then the rest must follow as effect.

Ours is to put the chemicals together, the crystallization comes in the law of nature.[5]

My idea is first of all to bring out the gems of spirituality that are stored up in our books and in the possession of a few only, hidden as it were in monasteries and forests to bring them out; to bring the knowledge out of them, not only from the hands where it is hidden, but from the still more inaccessible chest, the language in which it is preserved, the incrustation of centuries of Sanskrit words. In one word, I want to make them popular. I want to bring out these ideas and let them be the common property of all, of every man in India, whether he knows the Sanskrit language or not. The great difficult in the ways is the Sanskrit language, this glorious language of ours, and this difficulty cannot be removed until, if it is possible the whole of our nation are good Sanskrit scholars. You will understand the difficulty when I tell you that I have been studying this language all my life and yet every new book is new to me. How much more difficult would it then be for people who never had time to study it thoroughly! Therefore the ideas must be taught in the language of the people.[6] Teach the masses in the vernaculars. Give them ideas; they will information, but something more will be necessary. Give them culture. Until you can give them that, there can be no permanence in the raised condition of the masses.[7]

At the same time Sanskrit education must go along with it, because the very sound of Sanskrit words gives a prestige, a power and a strength to the race.[8] Even the great Buddha made one false step when he stopped the Sanskrit language from being studied by the masses. He wanted rapid and immediate results; and translated and preached in the language of the day-Pali. That was grand; he spoke the language of the people and the people understood him. It spread the ideas quickly and made them reach far and wide. But along with that Sanskrit ought to have been spread. Knowledge came, but prestige was not there. Until you give them that, there will be another caste, created, having the advantage of the Sanskrit language, which will quickly get above the rest.[9]

Remember that the nation lives in the cottage.[9] Your duty at present is to go from one part of the country to another, from village to village, and make the people understand that mere sitting about idly won't do any more. Make them understand their real condition and say, 'O ye Brother, all arise! Awake! How much longer would you remain asleep!' Go and advise them how to improve their own condition and make them comprehend the sublime truths of the *shastras,* by presenting them in a lucid and popular way. Impress upon their minds that they have the same right to religion as the Brahmanas. Initiate, even down to the Chandalas, in these fiery *mantras.* Also instruct them in simple words about the necessities of life, and in trade, commerce, agriculture, etc.[10]

Centuries and centuries, a thousand years of crushing tyranny of castes, kings and foreigners have taken out all their strength. And the first step in getting Strength is to uphold the Upanishads and believe 'I am the Soul', Me the sword cannot cut; nor weapons pierce; me the fire cannot burn; me the air cannot dry; I am the Omnipotent. I am the Omniscient.'[11] These conceptions of the Vedanta must come out from the forest and the cave, they must come out to work at the bar and the bench, in the pulpit and in the cottage of the poor man, with the fishermen that are catching fish and with the students that are studying. They call to every man, woman and child, whatever their occupation, wherever they may be. How can the fishermen and all these carry out the ideas of the Upanishads? The way has been shown. Of the fisherman thinks that he is the spirit, he will be a better fisherman; if a student thinks he is the spirit, he will be a better student.[12]

The one thing that is at the root of all evils in India is the condition of the poor.[13] Suppose you open a free school in every village, still it would do no good, for the poverty in India is such that the poor boys would rather go to help their fathers in the fields or otherwise try to make a living than come to the school. Now if the mountain does not come to Mohammed, Mohammed must go to the mountain. If the poor boy cannot come to education, education must go to him. There are thousands of single minded, self-sacrificing *sannyasins* in our own country, going from village to village, teaching religion. If some of them can be organised as teachers of secular things also, they will go from place, from door to door, not only preaching but teaching also. Suppose two of these men go to a village in the evening with a camera, a globe, some map etc., they can teach a great deal of astronomy and geography to the ignorant. By telling stories about different nations, they can give the poor a hundred times more information through the ear than they can get in a lifetime through books.[14] Kindly their knowledge with the help of modern science.[15] Teach them History, Geography, Science, Literature and along with these the profound truths of Religion through these.[16]

Engrossed in the struggle for existence, they had not the opportunity for the awakening of knowledge. They have worked so long like machines and the clever educated section have taken so long like machines and the clever educated section have taken the substantial part of the fruits of their labour. But times have changed. The lower classes are gradually awakening to this fact, and making a united front against this. The upper classes will no longer be able to repress the lower, try they ever so much. The well-being of the higher classes now lies in helping the lower to get their legitimate rights. Therefore I say: set yourself to the task of spreading education among the masses. Tell them and make them understand, 'You are our brothers, a part and parcel of our bodies.' If they receive this sympathy from you, their enthusiasm for work will be increased a hundredfold.[17]

Three things are necessary for great achievements. First, feel from the heart. What is in the intellect or reason? It goes a few steps and thee it stops. But through the heart comes inspiration Love opens the most impossible gates. Feel, therefore my would-be patriots. Do you feel? Do you feel that millions and millions of the descendants of gods and of sages have become next-door neighbour to brutes? Do you feel that millions are starving to-day, and millions have been starving for ages? Do you feel that ignorance has come over the land as a dark cloud? Does it make you restless? Does it make you sleepless? Has it gone into your blood, coursing through your veins, becoming consonant with your heart-beats? Has it made you almost mad? Are you seized with the one idea of the misery of ruin, and have you forgotten all about your name, your fame, your wives, your children, your property, even your own bodies? Have you done that? That is the very first step.[18]

You may feel then; but instead of spending your energies in frothy talk, have you found any way out, any practical solution, to soothe their miseries, to bring them out of this living death? Yet that is not all. Have you got the will to surmount mountain-high obstruction? If the whole world stands against you, sword in hand, would you still dare to do what you think is right? If your wives and children are against you, if all your name dies, your wealth vanishes, would you still stick to it? Would you still pursue it and go on steadily towards your own goal? As the great King Bhartihari says, 'Let the sages blame or let them praise; let the Goddess of Fortune come or let Her go wherever She likes; let death come to-day or let it come in hundreds of years; he indeed is the steady man who does not move one inch from the way of truth.' Have you got that steadfastness? If you have these three things each one of you will work miracles.[19]

Let us pray, 'Lead, kindly Light'; a beam will come through the dark, and a hand will be stretched forth to lead us. Let each one of us pray day and night for the down-trodden millions of India who are held fast by poverty, priestcraft and tyranny; pray day and night for them. I care more to preach to them than to the high and the rich. I am no metaphysician, no philosopher, nay, no saint. But I am poor. I love the poor. Who feels for the two hundred millions of , men and women sunken for ever in poverty and ignorance? Him I call a *mahatman* who feels for the poor. Who feels for them? They cannot find light or education. Who will bring the light to them—who will travel from door to door bringing education to them? Let these people be your God—think of them, work for them, pray for them incessantly—the Lord will show you the way.[20]

REFERENCES

1. Complete Works of Swami Vivekananda, Vol. V., p. 14.
2. *Ibid.*, Vol. V, p . 58.
3. *Ibid,* Vol. V, pp. 222-3.
4. *Ibid,* Vol. V, p. 482.
5. *Ibid.* Vol. IV, p. 362.
6. *Ibid,*Vol. III, p. 290.
7. *Ibid,* Vol. III, p. 291.
8. *Ibid,* Vol. III, p. 290.
9. *Ibid,* Vol. V, p. 90.
10. *Ibid,* Vol. V, p. 381.
11. *Ibid,* Vol. III, p. 244.
12. *Ibid,* Vol. III, p. 245.
13. *Ibid.* Vol. IV, p. 362.
14. *Ibid,* Vol. IV, p. 363.
15. *Ibid,* Vol. VII, p. 149.
16. *Ibid,* Vol. VII, pp. 148-9.
17. *Ibid,* Vol. VII, p. 149.
18. *Ibid,* Vol. III, pp. 225-6.
19. *Ibid,* Vol. III, p. 326.
20. *Ibid,* Vol. V, pp. 57-58.

10
An Appraisal

"The education which does not help the common mass of people to equip themselves for the struggle of life, which does not bring out strength of character, a spirit of philanthropy and the courage of lion – is it worth the name?"

—*Swami Vivekananda*

"We want that education by which character is formed, strength of mind is increased, the intellect is expanded, and by which one can stand on one's own feet".

—*Swami Vivekananda*

"We must have life-building, man-making, character-moulding, assimilation of ideas. If you have assimilated five ideas and made them your life and character, you have more education than any man who has got by heart a whole library."

—*Swami Vivekananda*

"The more the power of concentration, the more knowledge is acquired, because this is one and only method of acquiring knowledge."

—*Swami Vivekananda*

Alike T.P. Nunn and many other noted educationists of the modern world Swami Vivekananda firmly believed that knowledge is inherent in man, no knowledge comes from outside, it is all inside. In this context very often he gives the example of the discovery of the principle of gravitation by Newton whereby he means that the ideas of gravitation was already there in his mind. The falling of an apple on the ground from the tree was just stimulating factor. Therefore, he holds that "education is the manifestation of the perfection already in man."

Secondly he maintains that no one can teach anybody. The teacher spoils everything by thinking that he is teacher. Quoting the Vedanta he says that within man is all knowledge-even in a boy it is so—and requires only an awakening - and that much is the sole of a teacher. The New Education Policy (1986) also streamlines the role of a teach as facilitator or stage-setter. Further it adds that the one who inspires the students through his work and conduct (not simply by sermons) is the best teacher. According to Vivekananda, "Like fire in a piece of flint, Knowledge exists in the mind, suggestion is the friction which brings it out".

He lays more and more stress on character-formation, man-building and all round development of personality. To him the very essence of education is concentration of mind, not the collection of facts.

He was himself a good disciplinarian and particularly he advocated for 'self-discipline, which is a crux of all human values. Alike universal religion he laid more emphasis on universal ethics also. For him teacher's direct or indirect impact on student is very important, without which education is like a winter is Antaretica. Therefore, influence of the teacher on the student should be an integrat part of any good education.

He was a great admirer of the teacher-taught relationship prevailed in ancient India. The relationship was not only just cordial and smooth, but almost like the relationship of father and son. There are good number of glaring example to testify the testimony of the fact. According to him certain conditions are necessary in the taught and also in the teacher. The condition necessary for the taught are: purity, a real thirst for knowledge, modesty and perseverance. For the teacher purity in indeed, words and thought are very necessary. He must possess a high noble character.

He showed a great concern towards the education of the masses, particularly the downtroddens and backward communities for whom he was the first to coin the word 'daridra Narayan' (poor godly persons). The term was, later on, picked-up by Mahatma Gandhi, Vinoba Bhave and others.

According to him the chief cause of India's ruin has been the monopolising of the whole education and intelligence of the land among a handful of men. If we are to rise again, we shall have to do it by spreading education among the masses. He advocated to teach the masses in vernaculars, so that they may pick-up swiftly. At the same time Sanskrit education must go along with it as it is the repository of our cultural heritage. He was of the opinion that "Sanskrit words give a power, prestige and a strength to the race.

The culture and quality of the community is best known by the regard and respect it provides to its women-folk. Therefore, he pleaded for women education. In this contest he gave central place to the religion. All other training should be secondary to religion. According to him "religious training, the formation of character and observance of the vows of celibacy – there should be attended to. Women must develop a strong character. Women must be put in a position to solve their own problems in there own way. Our Indian women are as capable of doing it as any in the world.

In modern times there is co-existence of different ideologies and cultures, and hence a dynamic outlook and mental maturity are essential for adjustment and compromise. Vivekananda profusely supplies all these qualities and there is in him a happy blending of Idealism, Naturalism, Pragmatism and Realism in moderate degrees.

The real purpose of education in his view, is to make the individual aware of his innate potentialities. Here, he accepts the claims of idealism for the exaltation of human personality. He follows the naturalist trend in education when he pleads that the teachers' business is only to ensure the natural growth of the child by helping it to assimilate ideas rather than educating it. He becomes a pragmatist in suggesting that education should be activity-oriented and that aims and values can be separately viewed in the early stages of education. In accepting realism he considers the contribution of human realists, sense realists and social realists. The formation of character and exaltation of human personality are of supreme importance in his scheme.

The Significance of His Massage

Vivekananda provides a balanced philosophy of life synthesising spiritual idealism and social realism. Though a Sanyasin, he accepts the value of social and political changes if they are really meant for the welfare of the masses. His arguments are very original and meaningful. Instead of giving a textual discourse on the Gita he makes it the practical basis of a person's life and character.

Swamiji says that in a religion oriented country like India, education should be regarded as a means of spiritual realization. It is a fact that modern nationalism in India owes very much to western education and it is an ingredient of political socialization, and it is equally true that the nation is seriously lacking in self-discipline and self-respect. "The greatest misfortune of the Indian nation today is that large numbers of people have not realised the importance or self-discipline as an essential aspect of educational process."

It is to be reckoned here that Swamiji had gone deep into the social, political and cultural decline of India in his age and made a strong appeal that there should be economic efficiency, political stability, cultural advancement and a total awareness of rights and responsibilities. He saw the modern world saturated with the melody of scepticism, nihilism and power politics. He believed that they must be replaced by his master's grand ideals of universal love and selfless service.

The speeches and writings of Swami Vivekananda have their own irresistible impact on all the freedom loving people of the world. His greatest mission is to preach the gospel of Sri Ramakrishna with unmatched devotion and sincerity. He views all religions as one and suggests that the world should be made conscious of it through a sound system of education. He wants the intellectual elite to work for the poor and the depressed, and help them in the cultivation of right democratic attitudes and social justice. To him the political elite of a nation cannot have any objectivity in carrying out educational reforms. The growth of caste and communal loyalties would work only for satisfying sectional goals to the utter disregard of ideals and standards.

Though Vivekananda seems to be a little emotional in his utterances, he is at the same time a loving and sober-minded person. It is particularly significant that Swamiji spoke to different audiences under different contexts in his characteristic way and there cannot be any uniformity about them. But one can easily find that contemplation and devotion are unified in his personality. To him desire is misery and weakness is death. He was not only an ardent lover of freedom and a greater seer with an international message, but also a social reformer, patriot and prophet of India, modernising the nation for the attainment of social and cultural harmony. It would be a mistake to think of him merely as an Indian; he is for the entire humanity and his message is eternal.

Cultural Components

Swami Vivekananda laid more and stress on cultural components. According to him for good education cultural components are essential ingredients. In the modern time also our educationists are also realising that the basic emphasis in interlinking education and culture should be on the development of a child's personality particularly in terms of helping the child to discover his latent talent and to express it creatively. New Education Policy (1986) also envisaged development of a progressive sequence from the pre-primary stage to the university level. In this regard some features of the plan are as under:

- The means and material used for cultural exposure would be simple, inexpensive and related to their immediate environment.
- One a period of time, the concept of cultural neighbour-hood would be evolved, in which the community would be expected to play a significant role in terms of its help and involvement in various forms.

His dream was to make the great monastery, the mother house of Belur, a human "Temple of Knowledge," which indicates his cherished linkage between education and spiritualism.

11

Values and Beleifs of Swami Vivekanand

Swami Vivekanand was the awakened spirit of India in the real sense of the term. Through his wide travelling and interaction with the variety of strata of the society in the country and abroad he realised that the system of education in India is not in conformity with its basic theme, i.e., spiritualism particularly in his own time. Therefore, he suggested that religion and morality must get supreme consideration in education so that various moral, ethical, social and cultural values may be properly inculcated in the younger generation.

This chapter is aimed at bringing out the thought constructs of Swami Vivekanand upon which his social and educational philosophy is based. He insisted upon. 'Karma' (action) based on 'Dharma' (righteousness). "Work is worship" was his favourite dictum (found in one of the poems of carlyle. Carlyle says that "If you have got the work to do, youneed not ask any other boon from the Almighty".

In the tone of Karl Marx he said "Man is the meashre for everthing". Vivekananda's prime concern was man and his problems. His ideas and guidelines are very useful as far as solution of burning problems like national integration, poverty, illiteracy and emancipation of rural musses etc. are concerned.

Here we are reporoducing various values and beliefs cherished by him from the variety of works of Swami Vivekanand. Into the brackets volume number and page number are given for the convenience of the readers.

Belief

- Belief is no part of religion. We say religion is a superconscious state (V. 303).
- If you believe in a god, you can see him even now. (II. 372)
- Lord! How hard it is for man to believe in thee and thy mercies. (VI. 303)
- Whatever you believe, that you will be(III. 284)
- Those who are believers are heroes.(VI. 319)

Bhakti (devotion)

- The great quality of Bhakti is that it eleanses the mind (II.358)
- Hatred is a thing which greatly imedes the course of Bhakti. (III. 358)
- Bhakti can be more easily practised by persons in every condition of life. (III. 357)
- 'Pranidhana' is that sort of Bhakti in which without seeking results, such as sense enjoyuments etc. all works are indicated to that teacher of teachers.(III. 36)

Brahmacharya

- Is there a greater strength than that of brahmacharys. Purity my boy? (VI. 271)

Bravery

- The brave are always moral. (V.3) The brave alone can afford to be insecure. (VI. 110)
- None but the bravest deserves salvation. (I. 479).

The brave alone do great things, not the cowards. (V. 86)

Character

- Character is repeated bahits, and repeated habits alone can reform character (I. 208)
- It is character that cleaves its way through adamantine walls of difficulties. (IV. 367)
- It is character that pays everywhere. (V.51)
- Upon ages of struggle a character is built. Perfect love, the heart never reacting, this is what builds character. (VI. 135)
- Character is to be establish through a thousand stumbles. (VIII. 383)

Charity

- Test everthing, try everthing, and then believe it, and if you find it for the goodl of many, give it to all.(III.528)
- There is no higher virtue than charity. (IV.10)
- Charity never faileth. (VI. 121)
- The hand was made to give always. (IV.10)
- For the good of the many, for the happiness of the many great-souled men take their birth.(IV. 419)

Chastity

- Chastity is the life of a nation. (II. 101)
- Chastity is the corner-stone of all morality and of all religion. (VIII. 46)

Concertration

- The power of concerrtration is the only key to the treasure-house of knowledge. (II.391)
- Concertration is the essence of all knowledge. (VI. 123)

- Along with the development of concertration we must develop the power of detachment. (VI.38)

Discipline

- A sapling must be hedged about for protection; but when it becomes a tree, a hedge would be a hindrance. (VIII. 220)

Duty

- No duty is ugly. No duty is impure. (I.70)
- Each duty has its own place and according to the circumstances in which we are placed. We must perform our duties. (I.47)
- Duty of duty's sake, work for work's sake. (I.442)
- Duty is seldom sweet.
- Duty is sweet only through love, and love shines in freedom alone. (I.67)
- Only true duty is to be unattached and to work as free beings, to give up all work unto God. (I.103)
- Before reaching the highest ideal, man's duty is to resist evil, let him work, let him fight, let him strike straight from the shoulder. (I.39)
- Our duty is to encourage every one in his struggle to live upto his own highest ideal, and strive at the same time to make the ideal as near as possible to the truth. (I. 41)
- What is duty for one is not duty for another. (I.47)
- All our duties are His.(I.103)
- Ours are the duties. Let the fruits take care ofthemselves.(IV. 159)
- Every duty is holy, and devotion to duty is the highest form of the worship of God, it is certainly a source of great help in enlightening and emancipating the

deluded and ignorance-encumbered souls of the Buddhas-the bound ones. (V.240)

Equallity

- True equality has never been and can never be on earth. (I.113)
- No privilege for anyone, equal chances for all let everyone be taught that divine is within and everyone will work out his own salvation. (III.246)

Faith

- Faith is no belief, it is the grasp on the ultimate, and illumination. (VII. 60)
- He who has no faith in him self can never have faith in God.(I.38)
- A man must not only have faith but intellectual faith too. (V. 244)
- Faith is onr of the potent factors of huminity and of all religion. (III.444)
- It is faith that makes a lion of a man. (V.99)
- The essence of our faith consists somply in this freedom of the Ishto (V. 235)
- So long as you have faith in your Guru nothing will be able to obstruet your way. (V. 106)

Freedom

- The goal of the soul is freedom. (III. 127)
- Freedom is the song of soul. (I.335)
- Freedom is its(self 's) its nature, its birthright. (II.323)
- Freedom is its watchword. (II.323)
- Everywhere we see the assertion of freedom, this freedom of the soul.

- The search for freedom is the search of all religions. (II.400)
- This freedom is the goal towards which we all are moving. (II.256)
- Freedom of the motive of the universe, freedom is the goal. (V.434)
- Freedom is the one goal of all nature, sentient or insentient, and consciously or unconsciously, everything is struggling towards that goal. (I.109)
- All nature is crying through all the atoms for one thing-its perfect freedom. (IV. 241)
- Let us then be brave and sincere: whatever path we follow with devotion must take us to freedom. (VIII. 27)
- Fredom is to lose all illusion. (VII. 34)
- Liberty is the only condition of growth. (IV.346)
- Liberation consists in knowing. (IV.346)
- Our unity with the wonderful impersonality. (III.129)

Good

- The highest good is the realization of the self. (VIII.3)
- The road to the good is the roughest and steepest in the universe. (VIII.383)
- Contact with holy men is good. (VI.118)
- There are good and evil everywhere in the world. (VI. 54)
- It is only by doing good to others that one attains to one's own good and it is by leading others to Bhakte and Mukte that one attains them oneself. (VI.266)
- It is preferable to live on grass for the sake of doing good to others. (VI. 288)

- Disease and misfortune come to do us good in the long run. (VI. 429)
- What is goood for you may not be good for others. (VI.435)
- Doing good is not always smooth. (VIII. 511)
- There is no good in store so long as malice and jealousy and egotism will prevail. (VI.304)
- Goodness is strength. (IV.133)
- Truth is infinitely more weighty than untruth, so is goodness. (V.65)

Grace

- There is no condition in grace. (VI. 482)
- The wind of his grace is always blowing, what you need to do is to unfurl your sail. (VI. 481)
- Those who are pure always in body, mind and speech, who have strong devotion, who discriminate between the real and the unreal, who persever in meditaiton and contemplation-upon whom alone the grace of the Lord descends.(VI. 481)
- He on whom his grace descends, in a moment goes beyond all law. (VI. 482)

Happiness

- If I am unhappy, it has been of my own making , and that everything shows that I can be happy, if I will. (III.125)
- There is no happiness higher than what a man obtains by the attitude of non-offensiveness, to all creation. (I. 189)
- Happiness belongs to him who knows this oneness, who knows he is one with the universe. (I.374)
- The animal has its happiness in the senses, the man in

his intellect, and the God in spiritual contemplation. (I.186)

- Happiness is only found in the spirit. (II. 83)
- Real happiness is not in the senses; but above the senses. (IV. 283)

Help

- All search is vain until we begin to perceive that knowledge is within ourselves, that no one can help us, that we must help ourselves. (II.324)
- If we cannot help ourselves, there is none to help us. (I.478)
- All the help that has come was from writin yourselves. (II.324)
- If you want to help others, Your little self must go. (III. 431)
- In helping the world. We really help ourselves. (I.80)
- It is blasphemy to think that you can help anyone. (I.44)

Holiness

- Whatever is old becomes holy. (II.159)
- Holiness is the greates power. (VI. 89)
- So long as holiness is thus supremely venerated India cannot die. (IV.160)

Humanity

- Every human being is a perfect being.(II.502)
- Human nature is very Conservative.(II.116)
- To serve humanity is to serve God.

Immortality

- The idea of immortality is inherent in man. (II. 32)

- Immortality and bliss are not to be acquired , we possess them already, they have been ours all the time. (II.350)
- By renunciation alone immortality was reached. (IV. 338)

Knowledge

- Pleasure is not the goal of man, but knowledge.(I.27)
- Knowledge is the goal of all life. (IV. 210)
- We are all of us struggling towards knowledge. (I.204)
- The real life of man consists of knowledge. (I.52)
- He who can become mad with an idea, he alone sees light. (I.177)
- All our knowledge is based upon experience. (I. 125)
- Instinct, reason, and inspiration are the three instruments of knowledge. (II. 389)
- Generalisation is the essence of knowledge. (IV. 380)
- Books are infinte in number, and time is short; therefore the secret of knowledge is to take what is essential. (I.236)
- Perception is our only real knowledge of religion. (VII. 59)
- It is practice first, and knowledge afterwards.(II.317)
- All knowledge depends upon calmness of mind. (VII.72)
- "No knowledge is possible without a teacher". (IV.431)
- No one can teach anybody. (V.366)
- The gift of knowledge is the highest gift in the world. (VII. 256)
- The first end of life is knowledge; the second end of life is happiness. (VI. 83)

- Knowledge and happiness lead to freedom. (VI.83)
- No action can give you freedom; only knowledge can make you free, Knowledge is irresistible; the mind cannot take it or reject it. (VII.54)
- Knowledge itself is a manufactured something , a combination; it is not reality. (I. 213)
- Knowledge itself is the highest reward of knowledge. (I. 130)
- Knowledge alone can make us perfect. (VII. 38)
- Knowledge is power. (I.144)
- The only value of knowledge is in the strenghtening, the disciplining, of the mind. (VI. 64)
- Is there a greater strength than that of knowledge? (VI. 325)
- Knowledge is objectification. (II. 134)
- Knowledge is a limitation, knowledge is objectifying. (II.82)
- Knowledge is, as it were, a lower step, a degeneration. (II. 82)
- All knowledge must stand on perception of certain facts, and upon that we have to build our reasoning. (II. 162)
- All human knowledge proceeds out of experience; we cannot know anything except by experience. (II.226)
- All knowledge is by reaction. (II.458)
- All knowledge and all power are within and not without. (I.422)
- Nobody ever created knowledge; man brings it from within. (II.339)
- There is no knowledge in nature; all knowledge comes from the human soul. (I.422)

- All knowledge is within us. (I.412)
- All knowledge is within (the) mind. (I. 509)
- Knowleddge is God. (VIII.137)
- All this knowledge is God himself. (VIII.137)
- Just as creation is infinite and eternal, without beginning and without end, so is the knowledge of God without beginning and without end. (III.119)
- Higher knowledge is thus clearly shown to be the knowledge of the Brahman. (III.85)
- In real knowledge there is no touch of work. (VII.212)
- Knowledge means finding this unity. (III.5)
- Knowledge is nothing but finding unity in the midst of diversity. (III.397j)
- Illumination born of discriminative reflection is the ultimate aim of Upanishadic knowledge. (VI.507)
- All knowledge is Veda, infinite as God is infinite. (VIII.136)
- All human knowledge is but a part of religion. (VII.103)
- Knowledge realises one. (IV.233)
- Knowing does not mean simply intellectual assent, it means realisation. (II.410)
- There is nothing higher than this knowledge of the Atman; all else is Mays, mere jugglery. (VI. 519)
- Knowledge does not come by sacnnce, but by seeking, worshipping, knowing the Atman. (VII.42)
- The goal of all is the knowledge of the Self, the realisation of this Self. (VI. 457)
- There is no other way to the knowledge of the Self but through Sannyasy. (VI. 506-7)
- All other kinds of knowledge are but non-knowledge in comparison with Self-knowledge. (IV. 404)

- When we know that we are the Self, then we are free. (VI. 84)
- Spiritual knowledge is the only thing that can destroy our miseries for ever. (I.52)
- Spiritual knowledge can only be given in silence like the dew that falls unseen and unheard, yet bringing into bloom masses of roses. (III.222)
- Of what use is knowledge if it does not show us the way to the Highest? (IV. 281)
- Supreme knowledge (can be learnt) even from the man of low birth.(IV. 338)
- The gross melts into the fine, physics into metaphysics, in every department of knowledge. (III.3)
- All knowledge is in the soul. (I. 514)
- The soul ldoes not know, It is knowledge itself. (I. 249)
- Whatever we know we have to know in and through Him. (II.133)
- Knowledge was not in matter, it was in man all the time . (II.339)
- Within man is all knowledge. (V. 366)
- It is only discovered—What was covered is uncovered. (VIII.136)
- Knowledge exists, man only discovers it. (VII. 79)
- Knowledge can never be created, it can only be discovered; and every man who makes a great discovery is inspired. (VII.39)
- Infinite knowledge abide within everyone in the fullest measure. (VIII.137)
- Past, present, and future knowleldge, all exist in all of us. (VIII.136)
- In knowledge is worship. (II.335)

- To separate ourselves utterly from matter and all belief in its realityis true Jnana. (VIII.5)
- No one who sells lhis knowledge is an Apta. (I.205)
- The Jnani has to be free from all form. (VIII. 11)
- The Jnani is a tremendous rationalist; he denies everything. (VIII. 11)
- All over the world, it is the wise man who enjoys the happiness of the world. (III. 20)
- All wise men think alike. (VIII. 160)
- The Jnani takes nothin for granted. (VIII. 11)
- Jnana-Yoga is thE surest way of arriving at facts. (VI. 42)

Language

- Language must be made like pure steel--turn and twist it any way you like, it is again the same—it clelaves a rock in twain at one stroke, without its edge being turned. (VI. 187-8)
- Language is the vehicle of ideas. (VI. 188)
- (Now) Human language is the attempt to express the truth that is within. (II.73)

Law

- Law is uniform. (I.197)
- Law is death. (III.516)
- Interdependence is the law of the whole luniverse. (II. 132)
- All love is life, it is theonly law of life; all selfishness is death, and this is true here or hereafter. (IV.367)
- Too many laws are a sure sign of death. (V.287)
- All things in nature work according to law. (VI. 92)
- A law is that which cannot be broken. (VI. 100)

- All nature is bound by, the law of its own action; and this law can never be broken. (VI. 99)
- Law exists so long as we are ignorant. (VI. 84)
- Evil actions leave none scot-free; Mother never spares anybody. (VIII. 499)
- Yesterday, competition was the law. Today, co-operation is the law. Tomorrow there is no law. (VIII. 223)
- The eternal law is self-sacrifice, not self-assertion. (VIII.23)
- The law of karma is the law of causation. (VI. 92)

Leader

- It is a very difficult task to on the role of a leader. (VI. 284)
- The leaders of our societies have never been either generals or kings, but Rishis. (III.175)
- There is no allegiance possible where there is no character in the leader, and perfect purity ensures the most lasting allegiance and confidence. (VI. 135)
- There must not be a shade of jealousy or selfishness, then you are a leader. (VI. 284)
- First, by birth, and secondly, unselfish—that's a leader. (VI.284)
- A leader must be impersonal. (VIII.429)
- Not every one is born to lead. (VIII. 428)
- The best leader, however, is one who "leads like the baby". (VIII.428)

Lord

- The Lord Himself works incessantly and is ever without attachment. (I. 60)

- Whatever comes to you is but the Lord, the Eternal, the Blessed One. (II. 326)
- The Lord alone is true. (IV. 60)
- The Lord is the only One who never changes. (IV. 129)
- The Lord is the wealth of those who have nothing. (IV 294)
- Is not the Lord infinitely greater than all human help? (V. .57)
- The Lord is great. I know He will help me. (V. 16)
- It is the Lord who protects His children in the depths of the sea. (V. 51)
- Glory unto the Lord, we will succeed. (V. 17)
- Glory unto the Lord—march on, the Lord is our General. (V. 17)
- Is the Lord to be hoodwinked by idle talk?(VI. 253)
- The Lord provides everything. (VI. 284)
- The goldness of gold, the silverness of silver, the manhood of man, thewomanhood of woman, the reality of everything is the Lord. (VI. 378)
- The will of Vishweshwara, the Lord of the universe, will prevail—whatever that may be. (VIII. 283—84)
- Seek the Lord and getting Him we get all. (VIII. 27)
- The Lord is all blissfulness. (VIII. 134)
- Only the Lord is unchangeable land He is Love. (VIII. 400)
- He, the Lord of the universe, is in every one. (VIII. 135)

Love

- Love is the easiest and smoothest way towards the self surrender or subjection of thewill, and hatred, the opposite. (VI.378-79)

- Love is beyond time and space, it is absolute. (VII. 11)
- Love itself is the eternal, endless sacrifice. (VI. 76)
- Love is its own end. (VI. 71)
- Love can never be the means: it must bne the perfect end. (VI. 71)
- Love is always of the ideal. (VIII. 222)
- Love is struggle of a human Soul to find its complement its stable equilibrium its infinite rest. (V.426)
- Love is, therefore, the only law of life. (VI.320)
- Love is always thehighest ideal. (II.49)
- The perfect love is very rare in human relation. (VI. 144)
- This (love) is the one motive power in the universe. (II. 51)
- Love is the only form in which love in loved. (VIII.154)
- Love knows no bargaining. (III. 87)
- The only medium through which spiritual force can betransmitted is love. (III. 51)
- There is only one element in life which is worth having at any cost, and it is love. (V. 144)
- All hatred is "Killing the self by the self" ; therefore, love is the law of life. (VIII. 35)
- Love is the easiest of all, it waits for no logic, it is natural. (VII.10)
- There are no "rights" , all is love. (VIII. 23)
- Love opens the most impossible gates; love is the gate to all the secrets of the universe. (III. 225)
- Love alone is the fittestthing to survive and not hatred. (III. 188)
- Love was the most visible of all visible things.(III. 398)

- Whether we do good or evil, the propeller is love. (III. 365)
- All earthly love proceeds from the body. (V. 138)
- Where love isnot returned forlove, cold indifference is the natureal lresult. (III. 86)
- Mother represrnts colourless love thatknows no barter, love that never dies. (VI. 149)
- Every act of love brings happiness. (I. 57)
- Real love makies us unattached. (I. 58)
- Unattached love will not hurt you. (I.442)
- Love matter and you become matter.(I.499)
- If you love, that love will come back to you, completing the circle. (I. 196)
- Prema is love, it leads to heaven.(VI.116)
- The last and highest manifestation of Prana is love. (VI. 129)
- We only love that which understands love, thatwhich drawsourlove. (VI. 51)
- Pure love has no motive. (VI.90)
- Kindness and love can buy you the whole world. (VI. 404)
- None lives, my boys, but he who loves. (IV. 367)
- We must love all. (IV. 221)
- Love, Love—that 's the one thing, the sole treasure. (IV. 494)
- The real helpn is feeling, love. (II. 307)
- Salvation is in work and love. (VIII. 240)
- The way of all ways torealisation is love. (VIII. 258)
- In the highest love, union is only of the spirit. (VIII.221)

- Love immense and infinite, broad as the sky and deep as the ocean—this is the one great gain in life. Blessed is he who gets it. (V.144)
- Good results can be produced only through love, through sympathy. (III. 198)
- The love of the whole includes the love of the parts. (III. 92)
- None but men of great renunciation, none but mighty giants among men, have a right to that Love Divine. (V 345)
- When love comes method dies. (V. 426)
- Every step that has been really gained in the world has been gained by love. (VII. 28)
- Love cannot be without a subject and an object. (VIII. 153)
- Merely to love is thesole requestthat true love has to ask. (VIII.201)
- Love shall win thevictory. (V. 51)
- Love makes no distinction between man and man. (V. 78)
- Love makes the whole universe as one's own home. (V. 78)
- Matter changed into spirit by theforce of love. (VIII. 429)
- Love never fails. (V. 51)
- Love never dies. (VIII.386)
- The only worship is love. (VIII. 331)
- Love comes and penetrates through the forms and sees beyond. (VI. 143)
- Love conquers in the long run. (VI.284)
- It is love that gives you the supernatural powers, love

that gives you Bhakti, love that gives illumination, and love, again, that leads to emancipation. (VI. 401)

- Love banishes all fear. (VIII. 154)
- Love knows no fear. (VI.71)
- Love questions not. (VI. 70)
- Love loves for the sake of love itself. (VIII.154)
- Therefore love for love's sake, because it is theonly law of life, just as you breathe to live. (VI.320)
- Love itself lis thehighest recompense of love. (II.393)
- Love is always the giver and never the taker. (II.48)
- Love knows no reward. (III. 88)
- Love is always for love's sake. (III. 88)
- My nature is to love Him, and therefore I love. (I. 12)
- To love because it is the nature of love to love is undeniably the highest and the most unselfish manifestation of love that may be seen in the world, (III.86)
- The first sign of love is when love asks nothing, (when it) gives everything. (VI.70)
- Love never asks, never begs. (VIII. 154)
- Begging is not the language of love. (III.88)
- There is not true love possible in the slave.(I.57)
- Beggar's love is no love at all.(VI.70)
- The first test of love is that it knows no bargaining. (II. 48)
- The reward of love is love. (II.53)
- Ordinarily human love is seen to flourish only in places where it is returned. (III.86)

- Prema cannot come while there is lust. (V. 346)
- Lust is the death of love. (V. 426)
- There can be no love so long as there is lust—even a speck of it, as it were, in theheart. (V. 345)
- With love, there is no painful reaction. (I.58)
- There is no act of love which does not bring peace and blessedness as its reaction. (I. 57-58)
- Love only brings a reaction of bliss. (I.58)
- Love is always a manifestation of bliss.(I.276)
- It requires no proofs to demonstrate the existence of the beloved to the lover. (III. 91-92)
- To the lover the beloved is the most beautiful being that ever existed. (II.49)
- Love is simply an expression of this infinite unity. (VIII.238)
- Love binds, love makes for that onenes. (II.304)
- The Infinite One comes within my fist under the bondage of love. (VI.259)
- All this is the manifestation of tha One Love more or less expressed. (II. 304)
- If one would expand hemust love, and when he ceases to love he dies. (II. 500)
- The highest expression of love is unification. (VII. 30)
- It is indeed very difficult to have an equal love for all, but without it there is no Mukti. (VI. 357)
- With the love of God will come, as its effect, the love of every one in the long run. (VIII. 258)
- "As oil poured from one vesel to another falls in an unbroken line, so, when the mind in an unbroken

stream thinks of the Lord, we have what is called Para-Bhakti or supreme love." (III. 85)

- Love must get to its right destination, it must go unto Him, who is really the infinite ocean of love. (III. 97)
- Our love must, therfore, be given to theHighest One who never dies and never changes, to Him in the ocean of whose love kthere is neitherebb nor flow. (III. 97)
- Wherever there is love, it is He. (II.393)
- Love is existence, God Himself; and all this is the manifestation of that One Love, more or less expressed. (II.304)
- The Love kof God is the only love that is higherthan a mother's love; all other are lower. (I.68)
- Nothing must stand between me and God except love. (VI. 76)
- Gopi-Lila (his disport with the cowherd maids) is the acme of the religion of love in which individuality vanishes and there is communion. (VI.110)
- When a person loves the Lord, the whole universe becomes dear to him, because it is all His. (III. 81)
- Men who cannot love God are no good, whatever work they do. (I. 513)
- Highest love forGod can never be achieved without renunciation. (VI. 505)

Meditation (Dhyana)

- The greatest help to spiritual lifeis meditation. (II. 37)
- Meditation is the means of unification of the subject and object. (VI. 91)
- Meditations means the mind it turned back upon itself. (IV. 235)

Mercy

- Mercy is heaven itself; to be good, we have all to be merciful. (I.59)

Obedience

- Everyone wants to command, and no one wants to obey. (III. 134)
- The first requisite for organization is obedience. (VI. 321)
- The first thing needed is obedience. (VI. 322)

Peace

- What can be a greater giver of peace than renunciation? (IV. 404)
- Flying from work is never the way to find a peace. (IV. 130)
- Blessed are the peacemakers for they shall enjoy the earth. (VIII. 93)

Perseverance

- One must persevere, so that grace may be received. (VI. 481)
- Preseverence will finally conquer. (II.152)
- It is only those who persevers to the end that succeed. (V.31)

Purity

- Perfect purity is the most essential thing. For only the pure in heartshall see God. (VIII. 34)
- Out of purity and silence comes theword of power. (VII. 16)
- Purity in thought, speech and act is absolutely necessary for any one to be religious. (III. 48)

- To attain this purity of heart means long struggle and constant practice. (IV. 436)
- If you think yourself pure, pure you will be. (III. 130)
- Internal purity is of greater value than external. (I. 261)
- If you are pure, if you are strong, you one man, are equal to the whole world. (VI. 145)

Reason

- Reason helps inspiration. (VII.41)
- To reach truth by reason alone is impossible (VI.42)
- Why was reason given to us, if we have to believe?(VI.12)
- Reason can go only to certain extent, beyond that it cannot reach. (I.150)
- It is better that mankind should become atheist by following reason than blindly believe in two hundred millions of gods on the authority of anybody. (II.336)
- Reason is the historian of the actions of thehuman being. (VII. 59)

Renunciation

- This is one great duty, this is renunciation. (II. 37)
- Renunciation is the very high basis upon which ethics stands. (II. 62)
- The Alpha and Omega isrenunciation. (III. 343)
- Renunciation is not aseeticism. (VIII. 226)
- Renunciation is thevery soul of upnishads.(VI. 507)
- Renunciation is the evolution of nature and the manifestation of the God within.(V. 281)
- To live in the world and not to be of it is the true test of renunciation. (V.272)
- Without enjoyment renunciation can never come. (V.447)

- Renunciation is always the ideal of every race. (VIII. 524)
- If you desire to attain God. You will have to renounce kama—kanchana (Lust and possession)

Reverence

- Reverence is a growth out of love, we can none of us revere him whom we donot love. (III.79)

Sacrifice

- No great work can be done without sacrifice. (IV. 352)
- Great things can be done by great sacrifice only. (V. 34)
- Sacrifice in the past has been the law, it will be, alas for ages to come. (VII.501)

Sadhana

- Voluntarily weakening the body is really no prescription forspiritual enlightenment.(III.69)
- Great convictions are the mother of great deeds.(V. 30)
- Those that persever will see the light sooner or later. (V. 14)
- To control our passoons we have to control them at their very roots, then alone shall we be able toburn out their very seeds. (I. 242)
- Unhealthy persons cannot be Yogis. (I. 221)
- Mirachs are only stumbling blocks. (I. 328)

Self—Reliance

- The great thing is to have faith in oneself even before faith in God; but the difficulty seems to be that we are losing faith in ourselves day by day. (V.223)

Self—Restrain

- You donot require any assistance to govern yourself, you are already self—restrained.(III.159)

Strength

- The best guide in life is strength. (I. 134)
- Strength is the medicine that the ignorant must have when oppressed by the learned. (II. 201)
- Strength is life. Weakness is death. (V. 409)

Success

- The degree of unselfishness markks thedegree of success everywhere. (V. 240)

Sympathy

- Without real sympathy we can never teach well. (VII. 99)

Tolerance

- Tolerance only-we preach and perform. (VI. 285)
- The world is waiting forthis grand idea of universal toleration. (III. 187)

Truth

- That which is true must be infinite and eternal. (I. 449)
- Through truth everything is attained. (I. 189)
- Truth alone triumphs, and this is true. (I. 502)
- We are always after truth, but never want to get it. (I. 439)
- Truth can never come to us as long as we are selfist. (I. 476)
- Truth is heaven, Bigotry is hall.(VI.123)

- Truth is the fruit of realisation;Therefore seek it within the soul. (VI. 82)
- The greatest truths are the simplest things in the world, simple as your own existence. (III. 225)
- Great truths are simple, because they are of universal application. (VI.35)
- Truth is often far from being comfortable.(VIII.14)
- Ignorance and bigotry can never crush truth.(VII.422)
- The infinite truth never to be acquired. It is here all the time undying and unborn.(VIII.135)
- Books may perish, nation may go down in a erash, but the truth is preserved. (VII.428)
- Truth cannot be partial, it is for the good kof all.
- All power of creation must stop and then you know the truth at once. (I. 453)
- Truth comes unto him who knows the secret of it. (VI. 88)
- The truth can be learnt from the lowest individual, no matter to what caste or creed he belongs. (V.209)
- Truth must have no compromise. (VII. 70)
- Everything can be sacrificed for truth, but truth cannot be sacrificed for anything. (V. 410)
- Not from error to truth, nor from bad to good, but from truth to higher truth, from godd to better, best. (IV. 371-72)
- Truth comes to those alone who worship at her shrine for her sake only, without shopkeeping. (IV. 258)
- Truth never comes where lust and fame and greed of gain reside. (IV. 394)
- One progresses from a smaller to greater truth.(V. 202)

- If in this hell of a world one can bring a little joy and peace even for a day into the heart of a single person that much alone is true.(V. 177)

Unity

- In the heart of things there is unity still.(II.153)
- To realise this unity is the end and aim of all meditation, and this is what yajnyavalkya was trying to explain to Maitreyi. (II. 422)
- Unity is the only thing that exists. (I. 432)
- All reasoning ends only in finding unity, so we first use analysis, then synthesis.
- Unity in variety is the plan of the universe. (II. 381)
- All variations are in one. (VIII. 6)
- He who says he is different from others, even by a hair's breadth immediately becomes miserable. (I. 374)
- There is, therfore, but one At man, one self, eternally pure, eternally perfect, unchangeable, unchanged. (II. 275)
- When a perfect unity is reached, that science has nothing more of principles to tell us. (VI. 10)
- The end and aim of all science is to finnal the unity, the one out of which the manifold is being manufactured, that One exizting as many. (I. 133)
- Call it (unity) God, Love, Spirit, Allah, Jehovah-it is the same unity that animates all life from the lowest animal to the noblest man. (V. 192)
- "One without a second" can have no second. (VIII. 7)

Unselfishness

- The whole idea of human life can be put into that one word, unselfishness. (I. 182)

- Unselfishness is more paying, only people have not the patience to practice. (I. 32)
- The goal of all nature is freedom, and freedom istobe attained only by perfect unselfishness, every thought, word, or deed that isunselfish takes ustowards the goal, and, as such, is called moral. (I. 110)
- All ethics, all human action and all human thought, hang upon this one idea of unselfishness. (I. 182)
- The perfectly unselfish man is the most successful. (II. 4-5)

Appendix I

1. What is Education?*

1. Education is the manifestation of the perfection already in man. (IV. 358)

2. What is education? Is it book-learning? No. Is it diverse knowledge? Not even that. The training by which the current and expression of will are brought under control and become fruitful is called education. Now consider, is that education as a result of which the will, being continuously choked by force through generations, is now well-nigh killed out; is that education under whose sway even the old ideas, let alone the new ones, are disappearing one by one; is the education which is slowly making man a machine? (IV. 490.)

3. The true education is not yet conceived of amongst us. I never define anything, still it may described as a development of faculty, not an accumulation of words, or, as a training of individuals to will rightly and efficiently. (V. 231.)

4. A child teaches itself. But you can *help* it to go forward in its own way. What you can do, is not of the positive nature, but of the negative. You can take away the obstacles, but knowledge comes out of its own nature. Loosen the soil a little, so that it may come out easily. Put a hedge round it; see that it is not killed by anything, and there your work stops. You cannot do anything else. The rest is manifestation from *within* its own nature. So with the education of a child. A child educates itself.

---

* Teaching of Swami Vivekananda, pp. 50-55.

You come to hear me, and when you go home, compare what you have learnt, and you will find you have thought out the same thing; I have only given it expression. I can never teach you anything; you will have to teach yourself, but I can help you perhaps in giving expression to that thought. (IV. 55.)

5. You see, no one can teach anybody. The teacher spoils everything by thinking that he is teaching. Thus Vedanta says that within man is all knowledge—even in a boy it is so—and it requires only an awakening, and that much is the work of a teacher. We have to do only so much for the boys that they may learn to apply their own intellect to the proper use of their hands, legs, ears, eyes, etc., and finally everything will become easy. (V. 366.)

6. Haven't you read the stories from the Upanishads? I will tell you one. Satyakama went to live the life of a Brahmacharin with his Guru. The Guru gave into his charge some cows and sent him away to the forest with them. Many months passed by, and when Satyakama saw that the number of cows was doubled, he thought or returning to his Guru. On his way back, one of the bulls, the fire, and some other animals gave him instruction about the Highest Brahman. When the disciple came back, the Guru at once saw by a mere glance at his face that the disciple had learnt the knowledge of the Supreme Brahman. Now, the moral this story is meant to teach is that true education is gained by living in constant communion with Nature. (V. 369.)

7. To me the very essence of education is concentration of mind, not the collecting of facts. If I had to do my education over again, and had any voice in the matter, I would not study facts at all. I would develop the power of concentration and detachment, and then with a perfect instrument I could collect facts at will. Side by side, in the child, should be developed the power of concentration and detachment. (VI. 38-39.)

8. Well, you consider a man as educated if only he can pass some examinations and deliver good lectures. The education which does not help the common mass of people to equip themselves for the struggle for life, which does not bring out

strength of character, a spirit of philanthropy, and the courage of a lion—is it worth the name? Real education is that which enables one to stand on his own legs. The education that you are receiving now in schools and colleges is only making you a race of dyspeptics. You are working like machines merely, and living a jelly-fish existence. (VII. 147-48.)

9. Education is not the amount of information that is put into your brain and runs riot there, undigested all your life. We must have life-building, man-making, character-making, assimilation of ideas. If you have assimilated five ideas and made them your life and character, you have more education than any man who has got by heart a whole library. If education were identical with information, the libraries would be the greatest sages in the world and encyclopaedias the Rishis. (III. 302.)

10. Negative thoughts weaken men. Do you not find that where parents are constantly taxing their sons to read and write, telling them they will never learn anything, and calling them fools and so forth, the latter do actually turn out to be so in many cases? If you speak kind words to boys and encourage them, they are bound to improve to time. What holds good of children, also holds good of children in the region of higher thoughts. If you an give them positive ideas, people will grow up to be men and learn to stand on their own legs. (VII. 170.)

11. In language and literature, in poetry and in arts, in everything we must point out not the mistakes that people are making in their thoughts and actions, but the way in which they will gradually be able to do these things better. Pointing out mistakes wounds a man's feelings. We have seen how Sri Ramakrishna would encourage even those whom we considered as worthless, and change the very course of their lives thereby! His very method of teaching was a unique phenomenon. (VII. 170-171.)

12. Knowledge is inherent in man; no knowledge comes from outside; it is all inside. What we say a man "knows", should, in strict psychological language, be what he "discovers" or "unveils"; what a man "learns" is really what he "discovers",

by taking the cover off his own soul, which is a mine of infinite knowledge. We say Newton discovered gravitation. Was it sitting anywhere in a corner waiting for him? It was in his own mind; the time came and he found it out. (I. 28.)

13. All knowledge that the world has ever received comes from the mind; the infinite library of the universe is in your own mind. The external world is simply the suggestion, the occasion, which sets you to study your own mind, but the object of your study is always your own mind. The falling of an apple gave the suggestion to Newton, and he studied his own mind; he re-arranged all the previous links of thought in his mind and discovered a new link among them, which we call the law of gravitation. It was not in the apple nor in anything in the centre of the earth. (I. 28.)

14. All knowledge, secular or spiritual, is in the human mind. In many cases it is not discovered, but remains covered and when the covering is being slowly taken off we say "we are learning", and the advance of knowledge is made by the advance of this process of uncovering. The man from whom this veil is being lifted is the more knowing man; the man upon whom it lies thick is ignorant, and the man from whom it has entirely gone is all-knowing, omniscient. (I. 28.)

15. Like fire in a piece of flint, knowledge exists in the mind; suggestion is the friction which brings it out. (I. 28.)

16. No one was ever really taught by another; each of us has to teach himself. The external teacher offers only the suggestion which rouses the internal teacher to work to understand things. (I. 93.)

17. Education is not filling the mind with a lot of facts. Perfecting the instrument and getting complete mastery of my own mind [is the ideal of education]. If I want to concentrate my mind upon a point, it goes there, and the moment I call, it is free [again]. (I. 510.)

2

The Teacher Spirituality*

Every soul is destined to be perfect, and every being, in the end, will attain to that state. Whatever we are now, is the result of whatever we have been, or thought, in the past, and whatever we shall be in the future will be the result of what we do or think now. But this does not preclude our receiving help from outside; the possibilities of the soul are always quickened by some help from outside, so much so, that in the vast majority of cases in the world, help from outside is almost absolutely necessary. Quickening influence comes from outside, and that works upon our own potentialities, and then the growth beings, spiritual life comes, and man becomes holy and perfect in the end. This quickening impulse, which comes from outside, cannot be received from books, the soul can receive impulse only from another soul, and from nothing else. We may study books all our lives, we may becomes very intellectual, but in the end we find we have not developed at all spiritually. It does not follow that a high order of intellectual development always shows an equivalent development of the spiritual side of man; on the other hand, we find cases almost every day where the intellect has become very highly developed at the expense of the spirit.

Now, in intellectual development we can get much help

---

* Abridged edition of the Complete Works, 13th impression, Calcutta, 1995, pp. 45-54.

from books, but in spiritual development, almost nothing. In studying books, sometimes we are deluded into thinking that we are being spiritually helped; but if we analyse ourselves we shall find that only our intellect has been helped, and not the spirit. That is the reason why almost every one of us can *speak* most wonderfully on spiritual subjects, but when the time of action comes, we find ourselves so woefully deficient. It is because books cannot give us that impulse from outside. To quicken the spirit., that impulse must come from another soul.

That soul from which this impulse comes is called the Guru, the teacher, and the soul to which the impulse is conveyed is called the disciple, the student. In order to convey this impulse, in the first place, the soul from which it comes must possess the power of transmitting it, as it were, to another, and in the second place, the object to which it is transmitted must be fit to receive it. The seed must be a living seed, and the field must be ready ploughed, and when both these conditions are fulfilled, a wonderful growth of religion takes place. "The speaker of religion must be wonderful, so must the hearer be," and when both of these are really wonderful, extraordinary, then alone will splendid spiritual growth come, not otherwise. These are the real teachers, and these are the real students. Besides these, the others are playing with spirituality, just having a little intellectual struggle, just satisfying a little curiosity, but are standing only on the outward fringe of the horizon of religion. There is some value in that; real thirst for religion may thus be awakened; all comes in course of time. It is mysterious law of nature, that as soon as the field is ready, the seed *must* come, as soon as the soul *wants* religion, the transmitter of religious force *must* come. "The seeking sinner meeteth the seeking Saviour." When the power that attracts in the receiving soul is full and ripe, the power which answers to that attraction must come.

But there are great dangers in the way. There is the danger to the receiving soul of mistaking its momentary emotion for real religious yearning. We find that in ourselves. Many times in our lives, somebody dies whom we loved; we receive a blow; for a moment we think that this world is slipping between our fingers, and that we want something higher, and that we are going to be religious. In a few days that wave passes away, and we are left stranded where we were. We oft-times mistake such impulses for real thirst after religion, but so long as these momentary emotions are thus mistaken, that continuous, real want of the soul will not come, and we shall not find the "transmitter".

So, when we complain that we have not got the truth, and that we want it so much, instead of complaining, our first duty ought to be to look into our own souls, and find whether we *really* want it; in the vast majority of cases we shall find that we are not fit; we do not want; there was no thirst after the spiritual.

There are still more difficulties for the "transmitter". There are many who, though immersed in ignorance, yet, in the pride of their hearts, think they know everything, and not only do not stop there, but offer to take others on their shoulders, and thus "the blind leading the blind, they both fall into the ditch." The world is full of these; everyone wants to be a teacher, every beggar wants to make a gift of a million dollars. Just as the latter is ridiculous, so are these teachers.

How are we to know a teacher then? In the first place, the sun requires no torch to make it visible. We do not light a candle to see the sun. When the sun rises, we instinctively become aware of its rising, and when a teacher of men comes to help us, the soul will instinctively know that it has found the truth. Truth stands on its own evidences; it does not require any other testimony to attest it; it is self-effulgent. It penentrates into inmost recesses of our nature, and the whole universe stands up and says, "This is Truth". These are the very great teachers, but we can get help from the lesser ones also; and as we ourselves are not always sufficiently intuitive to be certain of our judgement of the man from whom we receive, there ought to be certain tests. There are certain conditions necessary in the taught, and also in the teacher.

The conditions necessary in the taught are purity, a real thirst after knowledge, and perseverance. No impure soul can be religious; that is one great condition; purity in every way is absolutely necessary. The other condition is, a real thirst after knowledge. Who *wants*? That is the question. We get whatever we want—that is an old, old law. He who wants, gets. To want religion is a very difficult thing, not so easy as we generally think. Then we always forget that religion does not consist in hearing talks, or in reading books, but it is a continuous struggle, a grappling with our own nature, a continuous fight, - till the victory is achieved. It is not a question of one or two days, of years, or of lives, but it may be hundreds of lifetimes, and you must be ready for that. It may come immediately, or it may not come in hundreds of lifetimes, and we must be ready for that. The student who sets out with such a spirit finds success.

In the teacher we must first see that he knows the secret of the scriptures. The whole reads scriptures, Bibles, Vedas, Korans, and others, but they are only words, external arrangement, syntax the etymology, the dry bones of religion. The teacher may be able to find what is the age of any book, but words are only the external forms in which things come. Those who deal too much in words, and let the mind run always in the force of words, lose the spirit. So the teacher must be able to know the *spirit* of the scriptures. The network of words is like a huge forest in which the human mind loses itself and finds no way out. "The various methods of joining words, the various methods of speaking a beautiful language, the various methods of explaining the dicta of the scriptures," are only for the the enjoyment of the learned. They do not attain perfection: they are simply desirous to show their learning, so that the world may praise them, and see that they are learned men. You will find that no one of the great teachers of the world went into these various explanations of texts; on their parts there is no attempt at "text-torturing", no saying "this world means this, and this is the philological connection between this and that word". You study all the great teachers the world has produced, and you will see that no one of them goes that way. Yet *they* taught, while others, who have noting to teach, will take up a word and write a three-volume book on its origin and use. As my Master used to say, what would you think of men who went into a mango orchard, and busied themselves in counting the leaves, and examining the colour of the leaves, the size of the twigs, the number of branches, and so forth, while only one of them had the sense to begin to eat the mangoes? So leave this counting of leaves and twigs, and this note-taking to others. That work has its own value in its proper place, but not here, in the spiritual realm. Men never become spiritual thought such work; you have never once seen a strong spiritual man among these "leaf-counters". Religion is the highest aim of man, the highest glory, but it does not require "leaf-counting." It you want to be a Christian, it is not necessary to know whether Christ was born in Jerusalem or Bethlehem or just the exact date on which he pronounced the Sermon on the Mount; you only require to *feel* the Sermon on the Mount. It not necessary to read who thousand words on when it was delivered. All that is for the enjoyment of the learned. Let them have it; say amen to that. Let *us* "eat mangoes".

The second condition necessary in the teacher is that he must be sinless. The question was once asked me in England by a friend: "why should we look to the personality of a teacher?—We have only to judge of what he says, and take that up." Not so. If a man wants to teach me something of dynamics or chemistry, or any other physical science, he may be of any character: he can still teach dynamics, or any other science. For the knowledge that the physical science require is simply intellectual and depends on intellectual strength; a man can have in such a case a gigantic intellectual power without the least development of his soul. But in the spiritual science it is impossible from first to last that there can be any spiritual light in that soul which is impure. What can such a soul teach? It knows nothing. Spiritual truth is purity. "Blessed are the pure in heart, for they shall see God. " In that one sentence is the gist of all religions. If you have learnt that, all that has been said in the past, and all that it is possible to say in the future, you have known; you need not look into anything else, for you have all that is necessary in that one sentence; it could save the world were all the other scriptures lost. A vision of God, glimpse of the beyond, never comes until the soul is pure. Therefore in the teacher of spirituality, purity is the one thing indispensable; we must see *first* what he is, and *then* what he *says.* Not so with intellectual teachers; there we care more for what he says than what he is. With the teacher of religion we must first and foremost see what he is, and then alone comes the value of the words, because he is the transmitter. What will he transmit, if he has not that spiritual power in him? To give a simile – If this heater here is hot, it can convey heat vibrations, but if not, it is impossible to do so. Even so is the case with the mental vibrations of the religious teacher which he conveys to the mind of the taught. It is a question of transference, and not of stimulating only our intellectual faculties. Some power real and tangible, goes out from the teacher and begins to grow in the mind of the taught. Therefore the necessary condition is that the teacher must be true.

The third condition is motive. We should see that he does not teach with any ulterior motive, for name, or fame, or anything else, but simply for love, pure love for you . When spiritual forces are transmitted from the teacher to the taught, they can only be conveyed through the medium of love; there is no other medium that can convey them. Any other motive, such as gain or name, would immediately destroy the conveying medium; therefore all must be done through love. One who has known God can alone be a teacher. When you see that in the teacher these conditions are fulfilled, you are safe; it they are not fulfilled, it is unwise to accept him. There is a great risk, if he cannot convey goodness; of his conveying wickedness, sometimes. This must be guarded against; therefore it naturally follows that we cannot be taught by anybody and everybody.

The preaching of sermons by brooks and stones may be true as a poetical figure, but no one can preach a single, grain of truth until he has it in himself. To whom do the brooks preach sermons? To that human soul only, whose lotus of life has already opened. When the heart has been opened, it can receive teaching from the brooks, or the stones, it can get some religion teaching from all these, but the unopened heart will see nothing but brooks and rolling stones. A blind man may come to a museum, but he comes and goes only; if he is to see, his eyes must first be opened. This eye-opener of religion is the teacher. With the teacher, therefore, our relationship is that of ancestor and descendant; the teacher is the spiritual ancestor, and the disciple is the spiritual descendant. It is all very well to talk of liberty and independence, but without humility, submission, veneration, and faith, there will not be any religion. It is a significant fact that where this relation still exists between the teacher and the taught, there alone gigantic spiritual souls grow, but in those who have thrown it off, religion is made into a diversion. In nations and churches where this relation between teacher and taught is not maintained, spirituality is almost an unknown quantity. It never comes without that feeling; there is no one to transmit, and no one to be transmitted to, because they are all independent. Of whom can they learn? And if they come to learn, they come to *buy* learning. Give me a dollar's worth of religion; cannot I pay a dollar for it? Religion cannot be got that way.

There is nothing higher and holier than the knowledge which comes to the soul transmitted buy a spiritual teacher. If a man has become a perfect Yogi, it come by itself, but it cannot be got in book. You may go and knock your head against the four corner of the world, seek in the Himalayas, the Alps, the Gaucasus, the Desert of Gobi or Sahara, or the bottom of the sea, but it will not come, until you find a teacher. Find the teacher, serve him as a child, open your heart to his influence, see in him God manifested. Our attention should be fixed on the teacher as the highest manifestation of God, and as the power of attention concentrates there, the picture of the teacher as man will melt away, the frame will vanish, and the real God will be left there. Those that come to truth with such a spirit of veneration and love—for them, the Lord of truth speaks the most wonderful words. " Take thy shoes from off thy feet, for the place whereon thou standest is holy ground." Wherever His name is spoken that place is holy. How much more so is a man who speaks His name, and with what veneration ought we to approach a man out of whom come spiritual truths! This is the spirit in which we are to be taught. Such teachers are few in number, no doubt, in this world, but the world is never altogether without them. The moment it is absolutely bereft of these, it will cease to be, it will become a hideous hell, and will just drop. These teachers are the fair flowers of human life, and keep the world going; it is the strength that is manifested from these hearts of life that keeps the bonds of society intact.

Beyond these is another set of teachers, the Christs of the world. These Teachers of all teachers represent God Himself in the form of man. They are much higher; they can transmit spirituality with a touch, with a wish, which makes even the lowest and most degraded characters, saints in one second. Do you not read of how they used to do these things? They are not the teachers about whom I was speaking; they are the Teachers of all teachers, the greatest manifestations of God to man; we cannot see God except through them. We cannot help worshipping them, and they are the only beings we are bound to worship.

No man hath "seen" God, but as He is manifested in the Son. We cannot see God. If we try to see Him we make a hideous caricature of God. There is an Indian story that an ignorant man was asked to make an image of the God Shiva, and after days of struggle, he made an image of a monkey. So, whenever we attempt to make an image of God we make a caricature of Him, because we cannot understand Him as anything higher than man, so long as we are men. The time will come when we transcend our human nature, and know Him as He is; but so long as we are men, we must worship Him in man. Talk as we may, try as we may, we cannot see God except as a man. We may deliver great intellectual speeches, become very great rationalists, and prove that these tales of God are all nonsense, but let us come to practical common sense. What is behind this remarkable intellect? Zero, nothing, simply so much froth. When next you hear a man delivering great intellectual lectures against this worship of God, get hold of him and ask him what is his idea of God, what he means by "omnipotence", and "omniscience", and "omnipresent love," and so forth, beyond the spelling of the words. He means nothing, he cannot formulate an idea, he is no better than the man in the street who has not read a single book. That man in the street, however, is quiet and does not disturb the world, while the other man's arguments cause disturbance. He has no actual perception, and both are on the same plane. Religion is realisation, and you must make the sharpest distinction between talk and realisation. What you perceive in your soul is realisation. Man has no idea of the Spirit, he has to think of it with the forms he has before him. He has to think of the blue skies, or the expansive fields, or the sea, or something huge. How else can you think of God? So what are you doing, in reality? You are talking of omnipresence, and thinking of the sea. Is God the sea? A little more common sense is required. Nothing is so uncommon as common sense, the world is too full of talk. A truce to all this frothy argument of the world. We are by our present constitution limited and bound to see God as man. If the buffaloes want to worship God, they will see Him as a huge buffalo. If a fish wants to worship God, it will have to think of Him as a big fish. You and I, the buffalo, the fish, each represents so many different vessels. All these go to the sea to be filled with water according to the shape of each vessel. In each of these vessels is nothing but water. So with God. When men see Him, they see Him as man, and the animals as animal—each according to his ideal. That is the only way you can see Him; you have to worship Him as man, because there is no other way out of it.

Two classes of men do not worship God as man—the human brute who has no religion, and the Paramhamsa (highest Yogi), who has gone beyond humanity, who has thrown off his mind and body, and gone beyond the limits of nature. All nature has become his Self. He has neither mind nor body, and can worship God as God, as can a Jesus or a Buddha. They did not worship God as man. The other extreme is the human brute. You know how two extremes look alike. Similar is the case with the extreme of ignorance and the other extreme of knowledge; neither of these worships anybody. The extremely ignorant do not worship God, not being developed enough to feel the need for so doing. Those that has attained the highest knowledge also do not worship God—having realised and become one with God. God never worships God. Between these two poles of existence, if anyone tells you he is not going to worship God as man, take care of him. He is an irresponsible talker, he is mistaken; his religion is for frothy thinkers, it is intellectual nonsense.

Therefore, it is absolutely necessary to worship God as man, and blessed are those races which have such a "God-man" to worship. Christians have such a God-man in Christ; therefore, cling close to Christ; never give up Christ. That is the natural way to see God; see God in man. All our ideas of God are concentrated there. The great limitation Christians have is that they do not need other manifestations of God besides Christ. He was a manifestation of God, so was Buddha, so were some others, and there will be hundreds of others. Do not limit God anywhere. Pay all the reverence that you think is due to God to Christ; that is the only worship we can have. God cannot be worshipped; He is the immanent Being of the universe. It is only to His manifestation as man that we can pray. It would be a very good plan, when Christians pray, to say, "In the name of Christ". It would be wise to stop praying to God, and only pray to Christ. God understands human failings and becomes a man to do good to humanity. "Whenever virtue subsides and immorality prevails, then I come to help mankind," says Krishna. He also says, "Fools, not knowing that I, the Omnipotent and Omnipresent God of the universe, have taken this human form, deride Me, and think that cannot be." Their minds have been clouded with demoniacal ignorance, so they cannot see in Him the Lord of the universe. These great Incarnations of God are to be worshipped. Not only so, they alone can be worshipped, and on the days of their birth, and on the days when they went out of this world, we ought to pay more particular reverence to them. In worshipping Christ I would rather worship Him just as He desires; on the day of His birth I would rather worship Him by fasting than by feasting—by praying. When these are thought of, these great ones, they manifest themselves in our souls, and they make us like unto them. Our whole nature changes, and we become like them.

But you must not mix up Christ or Buddha with

hobgloblins flying through the air, and all that sort of nonsense. Sacrilege! Christ coming into a spiritualistic *seance* to dance! I have seen that pretence in this country. It is not in that way that these manifestations of God come. The very touch of one of them will be manifest upon a man; when Christ *touches* the whole soul of man will change, that man will be transfigured just as He was. His whole life will be spiritualised from every pore of his body spiritual power will emanate. What were the great powers of Christ in miracles, and healing, in one of His character? They were low, vulgar things that He could not help doing because He was among vulgar beings. Where was this miracle-making done? Among the Jews; and the Jews did not take Him. Where was it not done? In Europe. The miracle-making went to the Jews, who rejected Christ, and the Sermon on the Mount to Europe, which accepted Him. The human spirit took on what was true, and rejected what was spurious. The great strength of Christ is not in His miracles or His healing. Any fool could do those things, fools can heal others, devils can heal others. I have seen horrible demoniacal men do wonderful miracles. They seem to manufacture fruits out of the earth. I have known fools and diabolical men tell the past, present, and future. I have seen fools heal at a glance, by the will, the most horrible diseases. These are powers, truly, but often demoniacal powers. The other is the spiritual power of Christ, which will live, and always has lived, an almighty, gigantic love, and the words of truth which He preached. The action of healing men at a glance is forgotten, but His saying, "Blessed are the pure in heart," that lives today. These words are a magazine of power, inexhaustible, so long as the human mind lasts. So long as the name of God is not forgotten, these words will roll on and on, and never cease to be. These are the powers Jesus taught, and the powers He had. The power of purity; it is a definite power. So in worshipping Christ, in praying to Him, we must always remember what we are seeking. Not those foolish things of miraculous display, but the wonderful powers of the Spirit, which makes man free, gives him control over the whole of nature, takes from him the badge of slavery, and shows God unto him.

3

Education of Our Women

Disciple: What sort of education, do you think, is suited to our women?

Swamiji: Religion, arts, science, housekeeping, cooking, sewing, hygiene-the simple essential points in these subjects ought to be taught to our women. It is not good to let them touch novels and fiction. The Mahakali Pathashala is to a great extent moving in the right direction. But only teaching rites of worship won't do; there education must be an eye-opener in all maters. Ideal characters must always be presented before the view of the girls to imbue them with a devotion to lofty principles of Sita, Savitri, Damayanti, Lilavati, Khana, and Mira should be brought home to their minds, and they should be inspired to mould their own lives in the light of these.[1]

But know for certain that absolutely nothing can be done to improve the state of things, unless there is spread of education first among the women and the masses. And so I have it in my mind to train up some Brahmacharins and Brahmacharinis, the former of whom will eventually take the vow of Sannyasa and try to carry the light of education among the masses from village to village, throughout the country, while the latter will do the same among women. But the whole work must be done in the style of your own country. Just as centres have to be started for teaching women. Brahmacharinis of education and character should take up the task of teaching at these different centres. History and the Puranas, housekeeping and the arts, the duties of home life and principles that make for the development of an ideal character, have to be taught with the help of modern science, and the female student must be trained up in ethical and spiritual life. We must see to their growing up as ideal mothers will make further progress in the virtues that distinguish the mothers. It is only in the homes of educated and pious mothers that great men are born. And you have reduced your women to something like manufacturing machines; alas, for heaven's sake, is this the outcome of your education? The uplift of the women, the awakening of the masses, must come first ,and then only can real good come about for the country, for India.[2]

My whole ambition in life is to set in motion a machinery which will bring noble ideas to the door of everybody, and then let men and women settle their own fate. Let them know what our forefathers as well as other nations have thought on the most momentous questions of life. Let them see specially what others are doing now, and then decide.[3]

Disciple:—Sir, history does not tell us of any Maths for women in India in ancient times. Only during the Buddhistic period one hears of Maths (nunneries) for women; but from it in course of time many corruptions arose . The whole country was overrun by great evil practices.

Swamiji:—It is very different to understand why in this country so much difference is made between men and women, whereas the Vedanta declares that one and the same conscious Self is present in all beings. You always criticise the women but say, what have you done for their uplift? Writing down Smritis etc. and binding them by hard rules, the men have turned the women into mere manufacturing machines! If you do not raise the women who are the living embodiments of the Divine Mother, don't think that you have any other way to rise.

Disciple:—Women are a bondage and a snare to men. By their Maya they cover the knowledge and dispassion of men. It is for this I suppose that scriptural writers hint that knowledge and devotion are difficult of attainment to them.

Swamiji:—In what scriptures do you find statements that women are not competent for knowledge and devotion? In the period of degradation, when the priests made the other castes incompetent to the study of the Vedas, they deprived the women also of all their rights. Otherwise you will find that in the Vedic or Upanishadic age Maitreyi, Gargi, and ladies of revered memory have taken the place of Rishis thought their skill in discussing about Brahman. In an assembly of a thousand Brahmanas who were all erudite in the Vedas, Gargi boldly challenged Yajnavalkya in a discussion about Brahman. When such ideal women were entitled to spiritual knowledge then, why shall not women have the same privilege now? What has happened once can certainly happen again. History repeats itself. All nations have attained greatness by paying proper respect to women. That country and that nation which do not respect women have never become great, nor will ever be in future. The principal reason why your race has so much degenerated is that you had no respect for these living images of Shakti. Manu says, "Where women are respected there the gods delight; and where they are not, there all works and efforts come to naught." There is no hope to rise for that family or country where there is no estimation of women, where they live in sadness. For this reason, they have to be raised first: and an ideal Math has to be started for them.

Disciple:—Sir, when you first returned from the West, in your lecture at the Star Theatre you sharply criticised the Tantras. Now by your supporting the worship of women as taught in the Tantras, you are contradicting yourself.

Swamiji:—I denounced only the present corrupted form of Vamachara of the Tantras. I did not denounce the Mother-worship of the Tantras, or even the real Vamachara. The purport of the Tantras is to worship women in a spirit of Divinity. During the downfall of Buddhism, the Vamachara become very much corrupted, and that corrupted form obtains to the present day. Even now the Tantra literature of India is influenced by those ideas. I denounced only these corrupt and horrible practices which I do even now. I never objected to the worship of women who are the living embodiments of Divine Mother, whose external manifestations appealing to the senses have maddened men, but whose internal manifestations such as knowledge, devotion, discrimination, and dispassion make man omniscient, of unfailing purpose, and a knower of Brahman. *'Saisha prasanna uarada nriam bhavati muktaye'*- "She when pleased becomes propitious and the causes of the freedom of man." Without propitiating the Mother by worship and obeisance not even Brahma and Vishnu have the power to elude Her grasp and attain to freedom. Therefore for the worship of these family goddesses, in order to manifest the Brahman within them I shall establish the women's Math.

Disciple:—It may be a good idea, but where will you get the women inmates? With the present hard restrictions of society, who will permit the ladies of their household to join your Math?

Swamiji:—Why so ? Even now there are lady- disciples of Shri Ramakrishna. With their help I shall starts this Math. The Holy Mother will be their central figure, and the wives and daughters of the devotees of Shri Ramakrishna will be it's first inmates. For they will easily appreciate the usefulness of such a Math. After that, following their example, many householders will help in this noble work.

Disciple:—The devotees of Shri Ramakrishna will certainly join this work. But I don't think the general public will help in this work.

Swamiji:—No great work has been done in the world without sacrifice. Who on seeing the tiny sprout of the banyan can imagine that in course of time it will develop into a gigantic banyan tree? At present I shall start the Math in this way. Later on you will see that after a generation or two people of the country will appreciate the a worth of this Math. The lady-disciples of mine will lay down their lives for it. Casting off fear and cowardice, you also be helpers in this noble mission and hold this high ideal before all. You will see, it will shed its lustre over the whole country in time.

Disciple:—Sri, please tell me all about your plan of this Math for women.

Swamiji:—On the other side of the Ganga a big plot of land would be acquired, where unmarried girls or Brahmacharini widows will live; devout married ladies will also be allowed to stay now and then. Men will have no concern with this Math. The elderly Sadhus of the Math will manage the affairs of this Math from a distance. There shall be a girls' school attached to this female Math, in which religion scriptures, literature, Sanskrit, grammar, and even some amount of English should be taught. Other matters such as sewing, culinary art, rules of domestic work, and up-bringing of children will also be taught, while Japa, worship and meditation etc. shall form an indispensable part of the teaching. Those who will be able to live here permanently, renouncing home and family ties, will be provided with food and clothing form his Math. Those who will not be able to do that will be allowed to study in this Math as day scholars. With the permission of the head of the Math the latter will be allowed even to stay the Math occasionally, and during such stay will be maintained by the Math. The elder Brahmacharinis will take charge of the training of the girl students in Brahmacharya. After five or six years training in this Math, the guardians of the girls may marry them. If deemed fit for Yoga and religion life, with the permission of their guardians they will be allowed to stay in this Math, taking the vow of celibacy. These celibate nuns will in time be the teachers and preachers of the Math. In villages and towns they will open centre and strive for the spread of female education. Through such devout preachers of character there will be the real spread of female education in the country. So long as the students will remain in association with this Math, the they must observe Brahmacharya as the basis idea of this Math.

Spirituality, sacrifice, and self-control will be the motto of the pupils of this Math, and service or Seva-Dharma the vow of their life. In view of such ideal lives, who will not respect and have faith in them ? If the life of the women of this country be moulded in such fashion, then only will there be the re-appearance of such ideal characters as Sita, Savitri and Gargi. To what straits the strictures of local usages have reduced the women of this country rendering them lifeless and inert, you could only understand if you visited the Western countries. You alone are responsible for this miserable condition of the women, and it rests with you also to raise them again. Therefore I say, set to work. What will it do to memorise a few religious books like the Vedas and so on?

Disciple:—Sir if the girl students after being trained in this Math marry, how will one find ideal characters in them? Will it not be better if the rule is made that those who will be educated in this Math shall not marry?

Swamiji:—Can that be brought about all at once? They must be given education and left to themselves. After that they will act as they think best. Even after marriage and entering the world, the girls educated as above will inspire their husbands with noble ideals and be the mothers of heroic sons. But there must be this rule that the guardians of the students in the female Math must not even think of marrying them before they attain the age of fifteen.

Disciple:—Sir, then girls will not command in society. Nobody would like to marry them.

Swamiji:—Why will not they be wanted in marriage? You have not yet understood the trend of society. Theses learned an accomplished girls will never be in want of bridegrooms. Society nowadays does not follow the texts recommending child-marriage nor will it do so in future. Even now don't you see?

Disciple:—But there is sure to be a violent opposition against this in the beginning.

Swamiji:—Let it be. What is there to be afraid of in that? Opposition to a righteous work initiated with moral courage will only awaken the moral power of the initiators the more. That which meets with no obstruction, no opposition, only takes men to the path of moral death. Struggle is the sign of life.

Disciple:—Yes, Sir.

Swamiji:—In the highest truth of the Parabrahman, there is no distinction of sex. We only notice this in the relative plane. And the more the mind becomes introspective., the more that idea of difference vanishes. Ultimately when the mind is wholly merged in the homogeneous and undifferentiated Brahman, then such ideas as this is a man or that a women do not remain at all. We have actually seen this in the life of Shri Ramakrishna. Therefore do I say that though outwardly there may be difference between men and women, in their real nature there is none. Therefore if a man can be a knower of Brahman, why cannot a women attain to the same knowledge? Therefore I was saying that if even one amongst the women become a knower of Brahman, then by the radiance of her personality thousands of women would be inspired and awakened to truth, and great well-being of the country and society would ensue. Do you understand?

Disciple:—Sir , your teachings have opened my eyes today.

Swamiji:—Not fully yet. When you will realise that all illumining truth of the Atman, then you will see that this idea of sex distinction has vanished altogether, then only will you look upon all women as the veritable manifestation of the Brahman. We have seen in Shri Ramakrishna how he had this idea of divine motherhood in every women, of whatever caste she might be, or whatever might be her worth. It is because I have seen this that I ask you all so earnestly to do likewise and open girls schools in every village and try to uplift them. If the women are raised, then their children will by their noble actions glorify the name of the country—then will culture, knowledge, power, and devotion awaken in the country.

Disciple:—But, Sir, contrary results appear to have come out of the present female education. With a smattering of education, they take merely to the Western modes of living, but it is not clear how far they are advancing in the spirit of renunciation, self-control, austerity, Brahmacharya, and other qualities conducive to Brahmajnana (knowledge of Brahman).

Swamiji:—In the beginning a few mistakes like that are unavoidable. When a new idea is preached in the country, some failing to grasp it properly, go wrong in that way. But what matters it to the well being of society at large? Well, those who are pioneers of the little bit of female educations that now obtains in the country, were undoubtedly very great hearted. But the truth is that some defect or other must creep into that learning or culture which is not founded on a religious basis. But now female education is to be spread with religion as its centre. All other training should be secondary to religion. Religious training, the formation of character, and observance of the vow of celibacy—these should be attended to. In the female education which has obtained up till now in India, it is religion that has been made a secondary concern; hence those defects you were speaking of have crept in. But no blame attaches therefore to the women. Reformers having proceeded to start female education without being Brahmacharins themselves have stumbled like that. Founders of all good undertakings before they launch on their desired work, must attain to the knowledge of the Atman through rigorous self discipline. Otherwise defects are bound to occur in their work.

Disciple:—Yes , Sir, it is observed that many educated women spend their time in reading novels and so on; but in East Bengal, even with education, women have not given up their religious, observances. Is it so here in this part?

Swamiji:—In every country, nations have their good and bad sides . Ours is to do good works in our lives and hold an example before others. No work succeeds by condemnation. It only repels people. Let anybody say what he likes, don't contradict him. In this world of Maya, whatever work you will take up will be attended with some defect- *'Sarvarambha hi doshena dhumenagnirvavritah'*— "All works are covered with defects as fire is with smoke. Every fire has a chance of being attended with smoke. But will you, on that account, sit inactive? As far as you can, you must go on doing good work.[4]

Education your women first and leave them to themselves; then they will tell you what reforms are necessary for them. In matters concerning them, who are you?[5]

Liberty is the first condition of growth. It is wrong, a thousand times wrong, if any of you dares to say, "I will work out the salvation of this women or child," I am asked again and again, what I think of the widow problem and what I think of the women question. Let me answer once for all – am I a widow that you ask me that nonsense? Am I a woman, that you ask me that question again and again? Who are you to solve women's problems? Are you the Lord God that you should rule over every widow and every women? Hands off! They will solve their own problems.[6]

REFERENCES

1. Complete Works of Swami Vivekananda, Vol. VI, pp. 493-94.
2. *Ibid.* Vol. VI, pp. 489-90.
3. *Ibid.* Vol. V, p. 29.
4. *Ibid.* Vol . VII, pp. 214-221.
5. *Ibid.* Vol. III, p. 115.
6. *Ibid.* Vol. VI, p. 246.

4
Ethics*

1. *That society is greatest, where the highest truth become practical.* That is my opinion, and if society is not fit for the highest truths, make it so, and the sooner, the better. Stand up, men and women, in this spirit, dare to believe in the Truth, dare to practise the Truth ! (II. 85).

2. Who know which is the truer ideal? The apparent power and strength, as held in the West, or the fortitude in suffering, of the East?

The West says: "We minimise evil by conquering it" India says: "We destroy evil by suffering, until evil is nothing to us, it becomes positive enjoyment" Well, both are great ideals. Who knows which will survive in the long run? Who knows which attitude will really most benefit humanity? Who knows which will disarm and conquer animality? Will it be suffering, or doing?

In the meantime, let us not destroy each other's ideals. We are both intent upon the same work, which is the annihilation of evil. You take up your method; let us take up our method. Let us not destroy the ideal. I do not say to the West: "Take up our method." Certainly not. The goal is the same, but the methods can never be the same. And so, after hearing about

---

* *Teachings of Swami Vivekananda,* Advaita Ashram, Calcutta, pp. 56-62.

the ideals of India, I hope that you will say in the same breath to India: "We know the goal, the ideal, is all right for us both. You follow your own ideal. You follow your method in your own way, and God speed you!" My message in life is to ask the East and West not to quarrel over different ideals, but to show them that the goal is the same in both cases, however opposite it may appear. As we wend our way through this mazy vale of life, us bid each other God-speed. (IV.76-77).

3. The work of ethics has been, and will be in the future, not the destruction of variation and the establishment of sameness in the external world, which is impossible, for it would bring death and annihilation- but to recognise the unity in spite of all these variations, to recognise the God within, in spite of everything that frightens , us, to recognise that infinite strength as the property of everyone in spite of all apparent weakness, and to recognise the eternal, infinite, essential purity of the soul in spite of everything to the contrary that appears on the surface. (I. 436.)

4. Coming to ethics, we find a tremendous departure. It is, perhaps, the only science which makes a bold departure from this fight. For ethics is unity: its basis love. It will not look at this variation. The one aim of ethics is this unity, this smeness. The highest ethical codes that mankind has discovered up to the present time, know no variation, they have no time to stop to look into it; their one end is to make for that sameness. The Indian mind, being more analytical–I mean the Vedantic mind–found this unity as the result of its anaysis, and wanted to base everything upon this one idea of unity. (I. 432.)

5. Karma-Yoga, therefore, is a system of ethics and religion intended to attain freedom through unselfishness, and by good works. The Karma-Yogi need not believe in any doctrine whatever. He may not believe even in god, may not ask what his soul is, not think of any metaphysical speculation. He has got his own special aim of realising selflessness; and he has to work it out himself. Every moment of his life must be realisation because he has to solve by mere work, without the help of doctrine or theory, the very same problem to which the Jnani

applies his reason and inspiration and the Bhakta his love. (I. III.)

6. In modern times this millennial aspiration takes the form of quality – of liberty, equality and fraternity. This is also fanaticism. True equality has never been and never can be on earth. How can we all be equal here? This impossible kind of equality implies total death . (I. 113.)

7. Yet this idea of realising the millennium is a great motive power. Just as inequality is necessary for creation itself, so the struggle to limit it is also necessary. If there were no struggle to become free and get back to God, there would be no creation either. It is the difference between these two forces that determines the nature of the motives of men. There will always be these motives to work, some tending towards bondage and others towards freedom. (1.115.)

8. That some will be stronger physically than others, and will thus naturally be able to subdue or defeat the weak, is a self-evident fact, but that because of this strength they should gather unto themselves all the attainable happiness of this life, is not according to law, and the fight has been against it. That some people through natural aptitude, should be able to accumulate more wealth than others, is natural ; but that on account of this power to acquire wealth they should tyrannise and ride roughshod over those who cannot acquire so much wealth, is not a part of the law, and the fight has been against that. The enjoyment of advantage over another is privilege, and throughout ages, the aim of morality has been its destruction. This is the work which tends towards sameness, towards unity, without destroying variety. (I. 435.)

9. Change is always subjective. All through evolution you find that the conquest of nature comes by change in the subject. Apply this to religion and morality, and you will find that the conquest of evil comes by the change in the subjective alone. That is how the Advaita system gets its whole force, on the subjective side of man. To talk of evil and misery is nonsense, because they do not exist outside. If I am immune against all

anger, I never feel angry. If I am proof against all hatred, I never feel hatred. (II.137-38).

10. Good and evil are only a question of degree: more manifested or less manifested. Just take the example of our own lives. How many things we see in our childhood which we think to be good, but which really are evil, and how many things seems to be evil which are good ! How the ideas change! How an idea goes up and up ! What we thought very good at one time we do not think so good now. So good and evil are but superstitions , and do not exist. The difference is only in degree. It is all a manifestation of that Atman; he is being manifested in everything; only, when the manifestation is very thick we call it evil; and when it is very thin, we call it good. (II. 420)

11. Ethics always says, "Not I, but thou." Its motto is, "Not self, but non-self." The vain ideas of individualism to which man clings when he is trying to find that Infinite Power, or that Infinite Pleasure through the senses, have to be given up, say the laws of ethics. You have to put yourself last , and others before you. The senses say, "Myself first." Ethics says, "I must hold myself last." Thus, all codes of ethics are based upon this renunciation; destruction, not construction, of the individual on the expression upon the material plane, nor is it possible or thinkable. (II. 62-63).

12. The great error in all ethical systems, without exception, has the failure of teaching the means by which man could refrain from doing evil. All the systems of ethics teach, "Do not steal!" Very good; why does a man steal? Because all stealing, robbing, and other evil actions, as a rule, have become automatic. The systematic robber, thief, liar, unjust man and women, are all these in spite of themselves! It is really a tremendous psychological problem. We should look upon man in the most charitable light. It is not so easy to be good. What are you but mere machines until you are free? Should you be proud because you are good? Certainly not. You are good because you cannot help it. Another is bad because he cannot help it. If you were in his position, who knows what you would have been ? The women in the street, or the thief in the jail, is the Christ that is

being sacrificed that you may be a good man. Such is the law of balance. All the thieves and the murders, all the unjust, the weakest, the wickedest, the devils, they all are my Christ! I owe a worship to the God Christ and to the demon Christ! That is my doctrine, I cannot help it. My salutation goes to the feet of the good, the saintly, and to the feel of the wicked and the devilish! The are all my teachers, all are my spiritual fathers, all are my Saviours; I may curse one and yet benefit by his failings; I may bless another and benefit by his good deeds. This is as true as that I stand here. I have to sneer at the women walking in the street, because society wants it! She, my Saviour, she whose street-walking is the cause of the chastity of other women! Think of that. Think men and women, of this question in your mind. It is a truth—a bare, bold truth! As I see more of the world, see more of men and women, this conviction grows stronger. Whom shall I blame? Whom shall I praise? Both sides of the shield must be seen, (II. 33-34.)

5

Stirring Utterances*

(Value-oriented Inspiring Tips)

Bold words and bolder deeps are what we want. Awake, great once! The world is burning with misery. Can you sleep? Let us call and call till the sleeping gods awake, till the God within answers to the call. What more is in life? What greater work?

Bear in mind, my children, that only cowards and those who are weak commit sin and tell lies. The brave are always moral. Try to be moral, try to be brave, try to be sympathizing.

Come be men ! Come out of your narrow holes and have a look abroad. See how nations are on the march! Do you love man? Do you love your country? Then come, let us struggle for higher and better things; look not back, no, not even if you see the dearest and nearest cry. Look not back , but forward!

India wants the sacrifice of at least a thousand of her young men—men, mind and not brutes.

Calm and silent and steady work, and no newspaper humbug, no name-making, you must always remember.

Can you become an occidental of occidentals in your spirit of equality, freedom, work, and energy, and at the same time a Hindu to the very backbone in religious culture and instincts?

---

* With courtesy from *'My India: India Eternal'*, Ramkrishna Mission Institute of Culture, Calcutta, pp. 144-54.

This is to be done and we will do it. You are all born to do it. Have faith in yourselves, great convictions are the mothers of great deeds. Onward for ever! Sympathy for the poor, the downtrodden, even unto death-this is our motto.

Onward, brave lads!

Three things are necessary to make every man great, every nation great:

1. Conviction of the powers of goodness.
2. Absence of jealousy and suspicion .
3. Helping all who are trying to be and do good.

Do not wait for anything. Do whatever you can. Build your hope on none.

Great things can be done by great sacrifices only. No selfishness, no name, no fame, yours or mine, nor my Master's even! Work, work the ideas, the plan, my boys, my brave, noble, good souls—to the wheel, to the wheel put your shoulders! Stop not to look back for name, or fame or any such nonsense. Throw self overboard and work.

'Wake up, stop not until the goal is reaches', say the Vedas. Up, up, the long night is passing, the day is approaching the wave has risen, nothing will be able to resist its tidal fury. The spirit, my boys, the spirit; the love, my children, the love; the faith, the belief; and fear not! The greatest sin is fear.

Do not be afraid of a small beginning, great things come afterwards. Be courageous. Do not try to lead your brethren, but serve them. The brutal mania for leading has sunk many a great ship in the waters of life. Take care especially of that, i.e. be unselfish even unto death, and work.

Work hard. Be holy and pure and the fire will come. Have faith that you are all, my brave lads, born to do great things! Let not the barks of puppies frighten you—no, not even the thunderbolts of heaven—but stand up and work!

Let people say whatever they like, stick to your own convictions, and rest assured, the world will be at your feet.

They say, 'Have faith in this fellow or that fellow', but I say, 'Have faith in your self first,' that's the way.

Say, 'I can do everything.' Even the poison of a snake is powerless if you can firmly deny it.

To work with undauted energy! What fear! Who is powerful enough to thwart you!...Fear ! Whom to fear, forsooth!

Renunciation!—Renunciation! — you must preach this above everything else. There will be no spiritual strength unless one renounces the world.

माभैः माभैः—Courage! Everything will come about by degrees. From all of you I want this that you must discard forever self-aggrandisement, faction-mongering, and jealousy. You must be all-forbearing, like Mother-Earth. If you can achieve this, the world will be at your feet.

Whatever other think or do, lower not your standards of purity, morality and love of God... No one who loves God need fear any jugglery. Holiness is the highest and divinest power in earth and in heaven.

I do not believe in a God or religion which cannot wipe the widow's tears or brings a piece of bread to the orphan's mouth. However sublime be the theories, however well-spun may be the philosophy—I do not call it religion so long as it is confined to books and dogmas. The eye is in the forehead and not in the back. Move onward and carry into practice that which you are very proud to call your religion, and God bless you!

No man, no nation, my son, can others and live; India's doom was sealed the very day they invented the word mlechchha and stopped from communion with others. Take care how you foster that idea. It is good to talk glibly about the Vedanta, but how hard to carry out even its least precepts!

A Sannyasin who has no idea of doing good to his fellow is a brute, not a Sannyasin.

I call him a traitor who, having been educated, nursed in luxury by the heart's blood of the downtrodden millions of toiling poor, never even takes a thought for them. Where, in what period of history your rich men, noblemen, your priests and potentates took any thought for the poor—the grinding of whose faces is the very life-blood of their power?

Who thinks of raising these sunken downtrodden millions? A few thousand graduates do not make a nation, a few rich men do not make a nation. True, our opportunities are less, but still there is enough to feed and clothe and make 300 millions more comfortable, nay, luxurious.

The only way is love and sympathy. The only worship is love.

I am thoroughly convinced that no individual or nation can live by holding itself apart from the community of others, and whenever such an attempt has been made under false ideas of greatness, policy, or holiness—the result has always been disastrous to the secluding one.

Give and take is the law, and if India wants to raise herself once more, it is absolutely necessary that she brings out her treasures and throws them broadcast among the nations of the earth, and in return be ready to receive what others have to give her. Expansion is life, contraction is death. Love is life and hatred is death.

Do any deserve liberty who are not ready to give it to others? Let us calmly and in a manly fashion go to work, instead of dissipating our energy in unnecessary frettings and fumings. I, for one, thoroughly believe that no power in the universe can withhold from any one anything he really deserves. The past was great no doubt, but I sincerely believe that the future will be more glorious still.

It is life to do good, it is death not to do good to others. Ninety per cent of human brutes you see are dead, are *ghosts*—for none lives, my boys, but he who loves. Feel, my children, feel; feel for the poor, the ignorant, the downtrodden, feel till the heart stops and the brain reels and you think you will go mad.

Be not afraid, my children. Look not up in that attitude of

fear towards that infinite starry vault as if it would crush you. Wait! In a few hours more the whole of it will be under your feet. Wait, money does not pay, nor name; fame does not pay, nor learning. It is love that pays; it is character that cleaves its way through adamantine walls of difficulties.

Bread! Bread! I do not believe in a God who cannot give me bread here, giving me eternal bliss in heaven! Pooh! India is to be raised, the poor are to be fed, education is to be spread, and the evil of priestcraft is to be removed. No priestcraft, no social tyranny! More bread, more opportunity for everybody!

Have fire and spread all over. Work, work. Be the servant while leading, be unselfish, and *never listen to one friend in private accusing another*. Have infinite patience, and success is yours.

Onward, my brave boys—money or no money—men or no men! Have you love? Have you God? Onward, and forward to the breach, you are irresistible.

Nothing shall be done in haste. Purity, patience, and perseverance are the three essentials to success and, above all, *love*. All time is yours, there is no indecent haste. Everything will come right if you are pure and sincere. We want hundreds like you bursting upon society and bringing new life and vigour of the Spirit wherever they go.

Pay no attention whatsoever to newspaper nonsense or criticism. Be sincere and do you duty. Everything will come all right. Truth must triumph.

You must give your body, mind, and speech to 'the welfare of the world'. You have read— मातृदेवो भव पितृदेवो भव — 'Look upon your mother as God, look upon your father as God,'— but I say, दरिद्रदेवो भव, मूर्खदेवो भव—the poor, the illiterate, the ignorant, the afflicted—let these be your God. Know that service to these alone is the highest religion.

Do not try to be a ruler. He is the best ruler who can serve well. Be True unto death. The work we want—we do not seek wealth, name or fame.

If you are really my children, you will fear nothing, stop at nothing. You will be like lions. We must rouse India and the whole world. No cowardice. I will take no nay. Do you understand? Be true unto death! The secret of this is Guru-Bhakti—faith in the Guru unto death!

Be the servant if you will rule. That is the real secret.

Remember ... we want both men and women. There is no distinction of sex in the soul... We want thousands of men, and thousands of women, who will spread like wild fire from the Himalayas to Cape Comorin, from the North Pole to the South Pole—all over the world. It is no use indulging in child's play—neither is there time for it. Let those who have come for child's play be off now, while there is time, or they will surely come to grief.

Let each one of us pray day and night for the downtrodden millions in India who are held fast by poverty, priestcraft, and tyranny—pray day and night for them. I care more to preach religion to them than to the high and the rich. I am no metaphysician, no philosopher, nay, no saint. But I am poor, I love the poor.

So long as the millions live in hunger and ignorance, I hold every man a traitor who, having been educated at their expense, pays nor the least heed to them! I call those men who strut about in their finery. Having got all their money by grinding the poor, wretches, so long as they do not do anything for those two hundred millions who are now no better than hungry savages!

Each nation has a main current in life; in India it is religion. Make it strong and the waters on either side must move along with it.

You must always remember that every nation must save itself; so must every men; do not look to others for help.

That you may catch my fire, that you may be intensely sincere, that you may die the heroes' death on the field of battle—is the constant prayer of Vivekananda.

I have not found a way that will please all, and I cannot but be what I am, true to my own self. 'Youth and beauty vanish, life and wealth vanish, name and fame vanish, even the mountains crumble into dust. Friendship and love vanish. Truth alone abides.'

Do not figure out big plans at first, but begin slowly, feel your ground, and proceed up and up.

One must work as the dictate comes from within, and then if it is right and good, society is bound to veer round, perhaps centuries after one is dead and gone. We must plunge heart and soul and body into the work. And until we be ready to sacrifice everything else to one *Idea* and to one alone, we *never, never* will see the light.

Was it ever in the history of the world that any great work was done by the rich? It is the heart and the brain that do it ever and ever and not the purse.

Know that every time you feel weak, you not only hurt yourself but also the cause. Infinite faith and strength are the only conditions of success.

Perfect sincerity, holiness, gigantic intellect, and an all conquering will. Let only a handful of men work with these, and the whole world will be revolutionized.

'Truth alone triumphs, not untruth. Through truth alone lies the way to Devayana (the way to the gods).' Those who think that a little sugar-coating of untruth helps the spread of truth are mistaken and will find in the long run that a single drop of poison poisons the whole mass… . The man who is pure, and who dares, does all things.

In religion lies the vitality of India, and so long as the Hindu race do not forget the great inheritance of their forefathers, there is no power on earth to destroy them.

Cultivate the virtue of obedience, but you must not sacrifice your own faith. No centralization is possible unless there is obedience to superiors. No great work can be done without this centralization of individual forces….

Give up jealousy and conceit. Learn to work unitedly for others. This is the great need of our country.

Infinite patience, infinite purity, and infinite perseverance are the secret of success in a good cause.

'Too many cooks spoil the broth.' In India the one thing we lack is the power of combination, organization, the first secret of which is obedience.

Go on bravely. Do not expect success in a day or a year. Always hold on to the highest. Be steady. Avoid jealousy and selfishness. Be obedient and eternally faithful to the cause of truth, humanity, and your country, and you will move the world. Remember it is the *person,* the life, which is the secret of power—nothing else.

The more the shades around deepen, the more the ends approach and the more one understands the true meaning of life, that it is a dream; and we begin to understand the failure of everyone to grasp it, for they only attempted to get meaning out of the meaningless.... 'Everything is evanescent, everything is changeful'—Knowing this, the sage gives up both pleasure and pain and becomes a witness of (the universe) this panorama without attaching himself to anything.

Neither numbers nor powers nor wealth nor learning nor eloquence nor anything else will prevail, but *purity, living the life,* in one word, *anubhuti,* realization. Let there be a dozen such lion-souls in each country, lions who have broken their own bonds, who have touched the Infinite, whose whole soul is gone to Brahman, who care neither for wealth nor power nor fame, and these will be *enough* to shake the world.

Let us work without desire for name or fame or rule over the others. Let us be free from the triple bonds of lust, greed of gain, and anger. And the truth is with us!

Are great things ever done smoothly? Time, patience, and indomitable will must show. I could have told you many things that would have made your heart leap, but I will not. I want iron wills and hearts that do not know how to quake. Hold on.

I hate cowardice; I will have nothing to do with cowards or political nonsense. I do not believe in any politics. God and truth are the only politics in the world, everything else is trash.

Purity, perseverance, and energy—these three I want.

Purity, patience, and perseverance overcome all obstacles. All great things must of necessity be slow.

Take courage and work on. Patience and steady work—this is the only way.

He who knows how to obey knows how to command. Learn obedience first.... We are all of us self-important—which never produces any work. Great enterprise, boundless courage, tremendous energy, and, above all, perfect obedience—these are the only traits that lead to individual and national regeneration.

Do you think there are *men* in our country, it is a *Golgotha*! There is some chance if you can impart education to the masses. Is there a greater strength than that of knowledge? Can you give them education? Name me the country where rich men ever helped anybody! In all countries it is the middle classes that do all great works. How long will it take to raise the money? Where are the *men*? Are there any in our country?

You must not throw cold water on anybody's project. Give up criticism altogether. Help all as long as you find they are doing all right, and in cases where they seem to be going wrong, show them their mistakes gently. It is criticizing each other that is at the root of all mischief. That is the chief factor in breaking down organizations.

No great work can be achieved by humbug. It is through love, a passion for truth, and tremendous energy, that all undertakings are accomplished. तत् कुरु पौरुषम्—Therefore, manifest your manhood.

We would do nothing ourselves and would scoff at others who try to do something—this is the bane that has brought about our downfall as a nation. Want of sympathy and lack of energy are at the root of all misery, and you must therefore give these two up.

No need of looking behind. FORWARD! We want infinite energy, infinite zeal, infinite courage, and infinite patience then only will great things be achieved.

He who is the servant of all is their true master. He never becomes a leader in whose love there is a consideration of high or low. He whose love knows no end, and never stops to consider high or low, has the whole world lying at his feet.

Religions of the world have become lifeless mockeries. What the world wants to character. The world is in need of those whose life is one burning love, selfless. That love will make every word tell like thunderbolt.

Be you holy and, above all, sincere and do not for a moment give up your trust in the Lord and you will see the light. Whatever is truth will remain for ever; whatever is not, none can preserve.

What I want is muscles of iron and nerves of steel, inside which dwells a mind of the same material as that of which the thunderbolt is made. Strength, manhood, Kshatra-Virya + Brahma-Teja.

Hold on to your own idea.... Above all, never attempt to guide or rule others, or, as the Yankees say, 'boss' others. Be the servant of all.

Know that talking ill of others in private is a sin. You must wholly avoid it. Many things may occur to the mind, but it gradually makes a mountain of a molehill if you try to express them. Everything is ended if you forgive and forget.

Another truth I have realized is that altruistic service only is religion, the rest, such as ceremonial observances, are madness—even it is wrong to hanker after one's own salvation. Liberation is only for him who gives up everything for others, whereas others who tax their brains day and night harping on 'my salvation', 'my salvation', wander about with their true well-being ruined, both present and prospective.

Doing good to others is virtue (Dharma); injuring others is sin. Strength and manliness are virtue; weakness and cowardice are sin. Independence is virtue; dependence is sin. Loving others is virtue; hating others is sin. Faith in God and in one's own Self is virtue; doubt is sin. Knowledge of oneness is virtue; seeing diversity is sin.

Persevere on, my brave lads. We have only just begun. Never despond! Never say enough!

I want each one of my children to be a hundred times greater than I could ever be. Everyone of you *must be a giant— must,* that is my word. Obedience, readiness, and love for the cause—if you have these three, nothing can hold you back.

Money and all will come of themselves, we want men, not money. It is man that makes everything, what can money do?— Men we want, the more you get, the better.

Men are more valuable than all the wealth of the world.

Love never fails, my son; today or tomorrow or ages after, truth will conquer. Love shall win the victory. Do you love your fellow men? Where should you go to seek for God—are not all the poor, the miserable, the weak, gods? Why not worship them first? Why go to dig a well on the shores of the Ganga? Believe in the omnipotent power of love. Who cares for these tinsel puffs of name? I never keep watch of what the newspapers are saying. Have you love?—You are omnipotent. Are you perfectly unselfish? If so, you are irresistible. It is character that pays everywhere. It is the Lord who protects His children in the depths of the sea. Your country requires heroes; be heroes!

Work unto death—I am with you, and when I am gone, my spirit will work with you.

Appendix II
World Thinkers on Vivekananda

The harmony of all religions which Ramakrishna Paramahansa accomplished in his life's endeavour, was the keynote of Swamiji's life. And this ideal again is the bedrock of the nationalism of Future India. Without this concept of harmony of religions and toleration of all creeds, the spirit of national consciousness could not have been build up in this country of ours full of diversities.

The aspiration for freedom manifested itself in various movements since the time of Rammohan Ray. This aspiration was witnessed in the realm of thought and in social reforms during the nineteenth century, but it was never expressed in the political sphere. This was because the people of India still remained sunk in the stupor of subjugation and thought that the conquest of India by British was an act of Divine Dispensation. The idea of complete freedom is manifest only in Ramakrishna-Vivekananda towards the end of the nineteeth century. "Freedom, freedom is the song of the Soul" –this was the message that burst forth form the inner recesses of Swamiji's heart and captivated and almost maddened the entire nation. This truth was embodied in his works, life conversations, and speeches.

Swami Vivekananda, the one hand, called man to be real man freed from all fetters and, on the other, laid the foundation for true nationalism in India by preaching the gospel of the harmony of religions.

Vinoba Bhave

Vivekananda not only made us conscious of our strength, he also pointed out our defects and drawback...India was then steeped in *tamas* (ignorance and unwisdom) and mistook weakness for non-attachment and peace. That is why Vivekananda went so far to say that criminality was preferable to lethargy and indolence. He made people conscious of the *tamasika* state they were in, of the need to break out of it and stand erect so that they might realize in their own lives the power of the Vedanta. Speaking of those who enjoyed the luxury of studying philosophy and the scriptures in the smugness of their retired life, he said football-playing was better than that type of indulgence. Through a series of, *obiter dicta*, he rehabilitated the prestige of India's soul force and pointed out to the t*amoguna* (unwisdom) that had eclipsed her. He taught us. 'The same Soul resides in each and all. If you are convinced of this, it is your duty to treat all as brothers and serve mankind.' People were inclined to hold that, thought all had equal right to the *tattvajana* (knowledge of the Spirit), the difference of high and low should be maintained in the day-to-day dealings and relations. Swamiji made us see the truth that *tattva-jnana*, which had no place in our everyday relationship with our fellow beings, and in our activities was useless and inane. He, therefore, advised us to dedicate ourselves to the service of 'Daridranarayana' (God manifested in the hungry, destitute millions) to their upliftment and edification. The word, 'Daridranarayana' was coined by Vivekananda and popularized by Gandhiji.

Romain Rolland

He [Vivekananda] was energy personified, and action was his message to men. For him, as for Beethoven, it was the root of all the virtues...

His pre-eminent characteristic was kingliness. He was a born king and nobody ever came near him either in India or America without paying homage to his majesty.

When this quite unknown young man of thirty appeared in Chicago at the inaugural meeting of the Parliament of Religions, opened in September 1893, by Cardinal Gibbons, all his fellow-members were forgotten in his commanding presence. His strength and beauty, the grace and dignity of his bearing , the dark light of his eyes, his imposing appearance, and from the moment he began to speak, the splendid music of his rich deep voice enthralled the vast audience of American Anglo-Saxons, previously prejudiced against him on account of his colour. The thought of this warrior prophet of India left a deep mark upon the United States.

It was impossible to imagine him in the second place. Wherever he went he was the first.. Everybody recognised in him at sight the leader, the anointed of God, the man marked with the stamp of the power to command. A traveller who crossed his path in the Himalayas without knowing who he was, stopped in amazement, and cried, "Shiva!..."

It was as if his chosen God had imprinted His name upon his forehead...

He was less than forty years of age when the athlete lay stretched upon the pyre...

But the flame of that pyre is still alight today. From his ashes, like those of the Phoenix of old, has sprung anew the conscience of India—the magic bird—faith in her unity and in the Great Message, brooded over from Vedic times by the dreaming spirit of his ancient race- the message for which it must render account to the rest of mankind.

Moving as were his [Vivekananda's] lectures at Colombo, and preaching to the people of Rameswaram—it was for Madras that he reserved his greatest efforts. Madras had been expecting him for weeks in a kind of passionate delirium...

He replied to the frenzied expectancy of the people by his Message to India, a conch sounding the resurrection of the land of Rama, of Shiva, of Krishna, and calling the heroic Spirit, the immortal Atman, to march to war. He was a general, explaining his *Plan of Campaign,* and calling his people to rise *en masse*:

"My India, arise !"...

"For the next fifty years...let all other vain Gods disappear for that time form our minds. This is the only God that is awake, our own race—everywhere His hands, everywhere His feet, everywhere His ears, He covers everything. All other Gods are sleeping. What vain Gods shall we go after and yet cannot worship the God that we see all round us, the Virat ?... The first of all worship is the worship of the Virat—of those all around us... These are all our Gods—men and animals, and first Gods we have to worship are our own countrymen..."

Imagine the thunderous reverberations of these words!...

The storm passed; it scattered its cataracts of water and fire over the plain, and its formidable appeal to the Force of the Soul, to the God sleeping in man and His illimitable possibilities! I can see the Mage erect, his arm raised, like Jesus above the tomb of Lazarus in Rembrandt's engraving : with energy flowing from his gesture of command to raise the dead and bring him to life....

Did the dead arise? Did India, thrilling to the sound of his words, reply to the hope of her herald? Was her noisy enthusiasm translated into deeds? At the time nearly all this flame seemed to have been lost in smoke. To years afterwards Vivekananda declared bitterly that the harvests of young men necessary for his army had no come from India. It is impossible to change in a moment the habits of a people buried in a Dream, enslaved by prejudice, and allowing themselves to fail under the weight of the slightest effort. But the Master's rough scourge made her turn for the first time in her sleep, and for the first time the heroic trumpet sounded in the midst of her dream the Forward March of India, conscious of her God. She never forgot it. From that day the awakening of the torpid Colossus began. If the generation that followed, saw, three years after Vivekananda's death, the revolt of Bengal, the prelude to the great movement of Tilak and Gandhi, if India today has definitely taken part in the collective action of organised masses, it is due to thé initial shock, to the mighty "Lazarus, come forth;" of the message from Madras.

This message of energy had a double meaning: a national and a universal. Although, for the great monk of the Advaita, it was the universal meaning that predominated, it was the other that revived the sinews of India.

His words are great music, phrases in the style of Beethoven, stirring rhythms like the march of Handel choruses. I cannot touch these sayings of his, scattered as they are through the pages of books at thirty years' distance, without receiving a thrill through my body like an electric shock. And what shocks, what transports must have been produced when in burning words they issued from the lips of the hero !

India was hauled out of the shifting sands of barren speculation where in she had been engulfed for centuries, by the hand of one of her own Sannyasins; and the result was that the whole reservoir of mysticism, sleeping beneath, broke its bounds and spread by a series of great ripples into action. The West ought to be aware of the tremendous energies liberated by these means.

The world finds itself face to face with an awakening India. Its huge prostrate body, lying along the whole length of the immense peninsula, is stretching its limbs and collecting its scattered forces. Whatever the part played in this reawakening by the three generations of trumpeters during the previous century – (the greatest of whom we salute, the genial Precursor: Ram Mohun Roy), the decisive call was the trumpet blast of the lectures delivered at Colombo and Madras.

And the magic watchword was Unity. Unity of every Indian man and women (and world-unity as well); of all powers of the spirit—dream and action: reason, love and work. Unity of the hundred races of India with their hundred different tongues and hundred thousand gods springing form the same religious centre, the core of present and future reconstruction. Unity of the thousand sects of Hinduism. Unity within the vast Ocean of all religious thought and all rivers past and present, Western and Eastern. For—and herein lies the difference between the awaking of Ramakrishna and Vivekananda and that of Ram

Mohan Roy and the Brahmo Samaj – in these days India refuses allegiance to the imperious civilisation of the West, she defends her own ideas, she stepped into her age-long heritage with the firm intention not to sacrifice any part of it, but to allow the rest of the world to profit by it, and to receive in return the intellectual conquests of the West. The time is past for the pre-eminence of one incomplete and partial civilisation. Asia and Europe, the two giants are standing face to face as equals for the first time. If they are wise they will work together, and the fruit of their labours will be for all.

This "greater India," this new India – whose growth politicians and learned men have, ostrich fashion, hidden form us and whose striking effects are now apparent –is impregnated with the soul of Ramakrishna. The twin star of the Paramahansa and the hero who translated his thoughts into action, dominates and guides her present destinies. Its warm radiance is the leaven working within the soil of India and fertilising it. The present leaders of India: the king of thinkers, the king of poets, and the Mahatma—Aurobindo Ghose, Tagore, and Gandhi—grown, flowered, and borne fruit under the double constellation of the Swan and the Eagle—a fact publicly acknowledged by Aurobindo and Gandhi...

As for Tagore, whose Goethe-like genius stands at the junction of all the rivers of India, it is permissible to presume that in him are united and harmonised the two currents of the Brahmo Samaj (transmitted to him by his father, the Maharshi) and of the new Vedantism of Ramakrishna and Vivekananda. Rich in both free in both, he has serenely wedded the West and the East in his own spirit. Form the social and national points of view his only public announcements of his ideas was, if I am not mistaken, about 1906 at the beginning of the Swadeshi movement, four years after Vivekananda's death. There is no doubt that the breath of such a Forerunner must have played some part in his evolution.

I was glad to hear Gandhi's voice quite recently—in spite of the fact that his temperament is the antithesis of Ramakrishna's or Vivekananda's—remind his brethren of the

International Fellowships, whose pious zeal disposed them to evangelise, of the great universal principle of religious "Acceptation", the same preached by Vivekananda...

At this stage of human evolution, wherein both blind and conscious forces are driving all natures to draw together for "co-operation or death", it is absolutely essential that the human consciousness should be impregnated with it, until this indispensable principle becomes an axiom: that every faith has an equal right to live, and that there is an equal duty incumbent upon every man to respect that which his neighbour respects. In my opinion Gandhi, when he stated it so frankly, showed himself to be the heir of Ramakrishna.

There is no single one of us who cannot take this lesson to heart. The writer of these lines—he has vaguely aspired to this wide comprehension all through his life—feels only too deeply at this moment how many are his shortcomings in spite of his aspirations; and he is grateful for Gandhi's great lesson—the same lesson that was peached by Vivekananda, and still more by Ramakrishna—to help him to achieve it.

Christopher Isherwood

Vivekananda was, as I said, profoundly moved by the realization India's poverty and state of her oppression under the British colonial rule. And he proposed a revolution. The spirit of this revolution enormously influenced Gandhi and influences Indian political thought to this day. Vivekananda in this sense is a great figure in Indian history, one of the very greatest historical that India has ever produced. But it must always be noted that Vivekananda's revolution, Vivekananda's nationalism, were not like the kind of revolution, the kind of nationalism, which we associate with other great leaders, admirable and noble as they may be. Vivekananda was far greater than that. In fact, when one sees the full range of his mind, one is astounded. Vivekananda looked toward the West, not simply as a mass of tyrants exploiting various parts of Asia, and other undeveloed areas, but as future partners, people who had very much to offer. At the same time, without any false humility, he faced the West and said, "we have fully as much and more to offer *you.* We offer you this great tradition of spirituality, which can produce, even now, today, a supremely great figure such as Ramakrishna. You can offer us medical services, trains that run on time, hygiene, irrigation, electric light. These are very important, we want them, and we admire some of your qualities immensely."

Once of the most enchanting things about Vivekananda is the way he was eternally changing sides when he was speaking to different people ; he could denounce the British in words of fire, but again he would turn on the Indians and say, "You cannot manufacture one pin, and you dare to criticize the British!" And then he would speak of the awful materialism of United States, and on the other hand, he would say that no women in the world were greater, and that the treatment of women in India was absolutely disgraceful. And so in every way, he was integrating, he was seeing the forces for good, the constructive forces, in the different countries, and saying, "why don't we exchange?" So Vivekananda's revolution was a revolution for everybody, a revolution which would in the long run be of just as much use to the British as to India. Vivekananda's nationalism, the call to India to recognize herself—this again was not nationalism in the smaller sense, it was a kind of super-nationalism, a kind of internationalism sublimated. You all know the story that Vivekananda was so found of, about the lion that was brought up with a lot of sheep. Now another lion comes out of the forest and the sheep all runs away, and the little lion that had been brought up thinking it's a sheep and runs away too, and now the pursuing lion grabs it, takes it over to a pool of water and says, "Look at yourself, you're a lion." This is what Vivekananda was doing to Indian people. He remarks in one of his letters , that the marvellous thing about all of the Western nations is that they know that they are nations. He said, jealousy is a curse of India. Indians cannot learn to co-operate with each other. Why can't they learn from the co-operation of Western nations with each other? I'm quoting all this because by considering all these different attitudes that Vivekananda took, one sees the immense scope and integrity of his good will. He was really on everybody's side, on the side of the west, and on the side of India, and he saw far, far into the future; his political prophecies are extremely interesting, and he said repeatedly, that the great force, which would finally have to be reckoned with was China. He also remarked on visiting Europe for the last time in 1900 that he smelled war everywhere, which was more than most professional statesmen did, at that time.

Will Durant

He [Swami Vivekananda] preached to his countrymen a more virile creed than any Hindu had offered them since Vedic days :

> It is a man-marking religion that we want... .Give up these weakening mysticisms, and be strong...For the next fifty years... let all other, vain gods disappear from our minds. This is the only God that is awake, our own race, everywhere His hands, everywhere His feet, everywhere His ears: He covers everything... . The first of all worship is the worship of those all around us...These are all our gods—men and animals; and the first gods we have to worship are our own countrymen.

It was but a step form this to Gandhi.

C. Rajagopalachari

Swami Vivekananda saved Hinduism and saved India. But for him we would have lost our religion and would not have gained our freedom. We therefore owe everything to Swami Vivekananda. May his faith, his courage and his wisdom ever inspire us so that we may keep safe the treasure we have received form him!

S. Radhakrishnan

We are today at a critical period not merely in the history of our country but in the history of the world. These are many people who think we are on the edge of an abyss. There is distortion of values, there is lowering of standards, there is widespread escapism ,a good deal of mass hysteria, and people think of it and collapse in despair, frustration, hopelessness. These are the only things which are open to us. Such a kind of lack of faith in the spirit of man is a treason to the dignity of man. It is an insult to human nature. It is human nature that has brought about all the great changes that have taken place in this world. And if there is any call which Vivekananda made to us, it is to rely on our own spiritual resources... Man has inexhaustible spiritual resources. His spirit is supreme, man is unique. There is noting inevitable in this world and we can ward off the worst dangers and worst disabilities by which we are faced. Only we should not lose hope. He gave us fortitude in suffering, he gave us hope in distress, he gave us courage in despair. He told us: 'Do not be led away by the appearances. Deep down there is a providential will, there is a purpose in this universe. You must try to co-operate with that purpose and try to achieve it.

E.P. Chelishev

Reading and re-reading the works the of Vivekananda each time I find in them something new that helps deeper to understand India, its philosophy, the way of the life and customs of the people in the past and the present, their dreams of the future...I think that Vivekananda's greatest service is the development in his teaching of the lofty ideals of humanism which incorporate the finest features of Indian culture...

In my studies of contemporary Indian literature I have more than once had the opportunity to see what great influence the humanistic ideals of Vivekananda have exercised on the works of many writers.... In my opinion, Vivekananda's humanism has nothing in common with the Christian ideology which dooms man to passivity and to begging God for favours. He tried to place religious ideology at the service of the country's national interests, the emancipation of his enslaved compatriots. Vivekananda wrote that the colonialists were building one church after another in India, while the Eastern countries needed bread and not religion. He would sooner see all man turn into confrimed atheists than into superstitious simpletons. To elevate man Vivekananda identifies him with God...

Though we do not agree with the idealistic basis of Vivekananda's humanism, we recognise that it possesses many features of active humanism manifested above all in a fervent desire to elevate man, to instil in him a sense of his own dignity, sense of responsibility for his own destiny and the destiny of all people, to make him strive for the ideals of good, truth and justice, to foster in man abhorrence for any suffering. The humanistic ideal of Vivekananda is to a certain degree identical with Gorky's Man with a capital letter.

Such a humanistic interpretation of the essence of man largely determines the democratic nature of Vivekananda's world outlook...

Many years will pass, many generations will come and go, Vivekananda and his time will become the distant past, but never will there fade the memory of the man who all his dreamed of a better future for his people, who did so much to awaken his compatriots and move India forward, to defend his much-suffering people from injustice and brutality. Like a rocky cliff protecting a coastal valley form storm and bad weather, from the blows of ill winds and waves, Vivekananda fought courageously and selflessly against the enemies of his motherland.

Together with the Indian people, Soviet people who already know some of the works of Vivekananda published in the USSR, highly revere the memory of the great Indian patriot, humanist and democrat, impassioned fighter for a better future for his people and all mankind.

Huang Xin Chuan

Vivekananda stands out as the most renowned philosopher and social figure of India in modern China. His philosophical and social thought and epic patriotism not only inspired the growth of nationalist movement in India, but also made a great impact abroad. In 1893, Vivekananda visited Canton and its neighbourhood. He noted his impressions of the visit in a letter addressed to the citizens of Madras. He had some knowledge and understanding of Chinese history and culture. He often cited and spoke highly of China in his writings and speeches. He made a prophecy that the Chinese culture will surely be resurrected one day like the 'Phoenix' and undertake the responsibility of the great mission of integrating the Western and the Oriental culture. His biographer Romain Rolland has narrated the evolution of Vivekananda's idea on his aspect. When Vivekananda went to America for the first time, he hoped that country would achieve this mission. But during his second visit abroad, he realised that he was deceived by dollar imperialism. He, therefore, came to the conclusion that America could not be an instrument to accomplish this task, but it was China which could do it.

Vivekananda had infinite sympathy for the Chinese people living under the oppression of feudalism and imperialism: and he pinned much hope on them. After his visit to China, he made a very interesting comment. He said: 'The Chinese child is quite a philosopher and calmly goes to work at an age when your Indian boy can hardly crawl on all fours. He has learnt the philosophy of necessity too well.' This shows Vivekananda's enormous sympathy towards the miseries of the children of China in the old society.

While explaining his visionary socialism Vivekananda made an interesting 'gospel'. He said that the future society would be ruled by the labouring people and that this would first take place in China. In 'Modern India' he said: 'But there is hope. In the mighty course of time, the Brahmin and the other highest castes, too are being brought down to the lower status of the Shudras and the Shudras are being raised to higher ranks. ...Even before our eyes, powerful China with fast strides, is going down to Shudrahood,... yet, a time will come when there will be the rising of the Shudra class, *with their Shudrahood,*

....a time will come when the Shudras of every country.... Will gain absolute supremacy in every society.... Socialism, Anarchism, Nihilism, and other like sects are the vanguard of the social revolution that is to follow'.

From the material cited above and his life and works, we can see at least that Vivekananda showed very much concern for, and sympathised with, the people of China who were living under the rule of feudalism and imperialism and placed great hopes on them. But we do not agree with B.N. Datta that the success of the Chinese and the Russian revolutions coming into being at concrete historical moments should be credited to the 'gospel' of Vivekananda. This would make him a divine mystique personality. We have seen that Vivekananda' approach to the laws of social developments was unscientific. However, it is not possible for any advanced thinker to make a correct prediction of the phases and events of the progress of history in every minute details. We should, therefore, appraise Vivekananda in the light of seeking truth from facts.

In conclusion, Vivekananda was the most eminent figure among the democratic patriots in India. He paid high tributes to our glorious ancient culture and loved the Chinese labouring people.

We pay homage to him.

K. M. Panikar

What gave Indian nationalism its dynamism and ultimately enabled it to weld at least the major part of India into one state was the creation of a sense of community among the Hindus to which the credit should to a very large extent go to Swami Vivekananda. This new Sankaracharya may well be claimed to be a unifier of Hindu ideology. Travelling all over India he not only aroused a sense of Hindu feeling but taught the doctrine of a universal Vedanta as the background of the new Hindu reformation... The Hindu religious movements before him were local, sectarian and without any all India impact. The Arya Samaj, the Brahmo Samaj, the Deva Samaj and other movements, very valuable in themselves, only tended further to emphasis the provincial character of the reform movements. It is Vivekananda who first gave to the Hindu movement its sense of nationalism and provided most of the movements with a common all-India outlook.

R. C. Majumdar

Vivekananda championed the cause of Hinduism in the Parliament of Religions held at Chicago (U.S.A.) in 1893 in connection with the celebration of the 400th anniversary of the discovery of America by Columbus. There, in the presence of the representatives of all the religions from almost all the countries in the world, the young monk from India expounded the principles of Vedanta and the greatness of Hinduism with such persuasive eloquence that from the very first he captivated the hearts of vast audience. It would be hardly an exaggeration to say that Swami Vivekananda made a place for Hinduism in the cultural map of the modern world. The civilized nations of the West had hitherto looked down upon Hinduism as a bundle of superstitions, evil institutions, and immoral customs, unworthy of serious consideration in the progressive world of to-day. Now, for the first time, they not only greeted, with hearty approval, the lofty principles of Hinduism as expounded by Vivekananda, but accorded a very high place to it in the cultures and civilizations of the world. The repercussion of this on the vast Hindu community can be easily imagined. The Hindu intelligentsia were always very sensitive to the criticism of the westerners, particularly the missionaries, regarding the many evils and shortcomings of the Hindu society and religion, as with their rational outlook they could not but admit the force of much of this criticism. They had always to be on the defensive and their attitude was mostly apologetic, whenever there was a comparative estimate of the values of the Hindu and Western culture. This sentiment was echoed and re-echoed in the numerous public addresses which were presented to Swami Vivekananda on his home-coming by the Hindus all over India, almost literally from Cape Comorin to the Himalayas. It was a great contribution to the growing Hindu nationalism.

On his return to India, Swami Vivekananda preached the spiritual basis of Hindu civilization and pointed out in his writings and speeches that the spirituality of India was not less valuable, nor less important for the welfare of humanity, than the much vaunted material greatness of the West which has dazzled our eyes. He was never tired of asking the Indians to turn their eyes, dazed by the splendour of the West, to their own ideals and institutions. By a comparative estimate of the real values of the Hindu ideals and institutions and those of the West he maintained the superiority of the former and asked his countrymen never to exchange gold for tinsels....

But Vivekananda was not prejudiced against the West nor insensible to the value of her achievements. He frankly admitted that Indian culture was neither spotless nor perfect. It has to learn many things from the West, but without sacrificing its true character.

Swami Vivekananda combined in himself the role of a great saint and fervid nationalist. He placed Indian nationalism on the high pedestal of past glory, and it embraced the teeming millions of India both high and low, rich and poor. He devoted his life to the awakening of national consciousness and many of his eloquent appeals would stir the national sentiments of India even today to their very depths....

Though an ascetic, Vivekananda was a patriot of patriots. The thought of restoring the pristine glory of India by resuscitating among her people the spiritual vitality which was dormant, but not dead, was always the uppermost thought in his mind....

This great *Sanyasin* who had left his hearth and home at the call of his spiritual *guru,* Sri Ramakrishna, and delved deeply into spiritual mysticism, was never tired of preaching that what India needs today is not so much religion or philosophy, of which she has enough, but food for her hungry millions, social justice for the low classes, strength and energy for her emasculated people and a sense of pride and prestige as great nation of the world. He made a trumpet call to all Indians to shed fear of all kinds and stand forth as men by imbibing *sakti* (energy and strength), by reminding them that they were the practices of the Divine according to the eternal truth preached by the Vedanta. The precepts and example of this great *Sanyasin* galvanized the current of national life, infused new hopes and inspirations, and placed the service to the motherland on a religious level....

Swami Vivekananda thus gave a spiritual basis to Indian nationalism. The lessons of the Vedanta and *Bhagavad-Gita* permeated the lives and activities of many nationalists, and many a martyr, inspired by his teachings, endured extreme sufferings and sacrifices with a cheerful heart, fearlessly embraced death, and calmly bore the inhuman tortures, worse than death, which were sometimes inflicted upon them....

R. G. Pradhan

Swami Vivekananda might well be called the father of modern Indian Nationalism; he largely created it and also embodied in his own life its highest and noblest elements.

A.L. Basham

Even for a hundred years after the birth of Narendranath Dutta, who later became Swami Vivekananda, it is very difficult to evaluate his importance in the scale of world history. It is certainly far greater than any Western historian or most Indian historians would have suggested at the time of his death. The passing of the years and the many stupendous and unexpected events which have occurred since then suggests that in centuries to come he will be remembered as one of the main moulders of the modern world, especially as far as Asia is concerned, and as one of the most significant figures in the whole history of Indian religion, comparable in importance to such great teachers as Shankara and Ramanuja, and definitely more important than the saints of local or regional significance such as Kabir, Chaitanya, and the many Nayanmars and Alwars of South India.

I believe also that Vivekananda will always be remembered in the world's history because he virtually initiated what the late Dr. C.E.M. Joad once called 'the counter-attack from the East'. Since the days of the Indian missionaries who travelled in South-East Asia and China preaching Buddhism and Hinduism more than a thousand years earlier, he was the first Indian religious teacher to make an impression outside India.

Michael Talbot

There are many parallel concepts between the ancient philosophers of the East and the emerging philosophers of the West. Certain concepts are so similar that it becomes impossible to discern whether some statements were made by the mystic or the physicist. Esalen Institute Psychologist Lawrence Leshan gives an example of such an indistinguishable statement: "The absolute (is) ....everything that exists. ....this absolute has become the universe ....(as we perceive it) by coming through time, space and causation. This is the central idea of (Minkowski) (Advaita). ....Time, space and causation are like the glass through which the absolute is seen and when it is seen ....it appears as the universe. Now we at once gather from this that in the universe there is neither time, space nor causation. ....what we may call causation begins, after, if we may be permitted to say so, the degeneration of the absolute into the phenomenal and not before."

The remark was originally made by mystic Swami Vivekananda in *Jnana Yoga*, but the fact that the names of the mathematician who first theorized that space and time are a continuum, Hermann Minkowski, and the greatest of the historical Brahmin sages, Advaita,* are interchangeable, demonstrates once again the confluence of mysticism and the new physics.

Vivekananda further expresses a view that has become the backbone of quantum theory: There is no such thing as strict causality. As he states, "A stone falls and we ask why. This question is possible only on the supposition that nothing happens without a cause. I request you to make this very clear in your minds, for whenever we ask why anything happens, we are taking for granted that everything that happened must have a why, that is to say, it must have been preceded by something else which acted as the cause. This precedence in succession is what we call the law of causation."

Suniti Kumar Chatterji

Vivekananda appeared to me immediately to be a man who was intensely moved by the suffering of Humanity, and particulary of Humanity in India. Some of his tirades against middle class and upper class societies in this matter moved us to the depths of our being. He discovered for us the greatness of Man, and particularly of men in the number walks of life who were the despised and the denied in our Indian society. At the same time, he brought home to us the value of Indian thought at its highest and pristine best, as in the *Vedanta*. He was able to convince us that what our ancestors had left in the *Vedanta* Philosophy was of permanent value, not only for us in India but also for the rest of Humanity. This put heart in us, and made us feel a new kind of elation as members of a people who have always had a mission and a sacred task to serve Humanity. The Hindus as a race were losing their nerve, and it was Vivekananda who helped us to regain this nerve which we were losing. There was a lot of unthinking and unsympathetic criticism of our ways and our life, particularly from among Christian missionaries of the older type, and this was demolished by Vivekananda. All this made us hold him very close to our heart, and to think of him as a great master and as a new kind of incarnation who came down to earth to lead us into the good life and the life of the strong man.

Vivekananda, in the first instance, knocked off a lot of nonsense in our Hindu social life, and drew our attention to the Eternal Verities and not to the ephemeral accidentals – social usages and such like—in our life. He was a sworn enemy of what we now call in India *Casteism*. *Untouchability* was something which he abhorred both as a *Sannyasin* and as a lay Hindu. He coined the world is very commonly used in our Indian English—"don't touchism." His heart overflowed with love and sympathy for the masses, whom he wanted to serve with religious zeal—serve as a believer in the *Vedanta* which sees God in all life. He coined a new world for our Indian languages—*Daridra-Narayana* or a "God in the poor and the lowly." This word has been accepted by the whole of India, and in a way it brings in a sense of responsibility for the average man. He has to look upon the poor and the humble, the suffering ones and the frustrated ones of society, as it they were deities incarnate or fragments of God, to serve whom was to serve God. Mahatma Gandhi's revival of the old expression which was used in Gujarati by the Vaishnava poets of Gujarat, namely, *Hari-jana* or " the Men of God" was a very fine expression: but *Daridra-Narayana* implied or brought in an element of a sense of duty which was enjoined upon man to serve the poor if they wanted to serve god.

Swami Vivekananda is looked upon as a great religious teacher, and indeed he made a definite contribution to the study of both Hindu religion and philosophy, and also in spreading a knowledge and appreciation of this philosophy and religion. His great works on aspects of *Vedanta* in theory and practice still inspire hundreds and thousands of enquires all over the worlds. But it has also been said that he was more a philanthropist, one who dedicated himself to the service of man, than a religious theorist or preacher. One need not seek to analyses Vivekananda's personality in this way. It is best to take the service of man as a form of serving God, for, form the point of view of all practical religion, God and Man are the obverse and reverse of the same medal. Vivekananda may be said to have been an innovator in two matters. As his great disciple Sister Nivedita suggested—he was the first to formulate the basic character of Hinduism as a system of thought and as a way of life in the modern age. This is the first thing we as Indians may note about Vivekananda. Secondly, Vivekananda may be said to have brought before the Western World a new point of view in religious thinking—a new approach to the problems of faith—which they needed very badly. To this also might be added as a pendant that Vivekananda, as one of the thought-leaders of modern India, gave the tone to modern India culture. He conceived of an Integration of all human religion and culture one entity claiming the homage of all and sundry.

Bibliography

Complete Works of Swami Vivekananda, Vols I to VII, Mayavati Memorial Edition 11th Edition, Advait Ashrama, 5, Dehi Entally Road, Calcutta-14.

Abhedanand Swami, *Great Saviours of the World*, Ramakrishna Vedanta Math, Calcutta, 1977.

Advait Ashram, *The Message of Swami Vivekananda*, Calcutta, 1966.

--, --, *Teachings of Vivekananda*, Calcutta, 1996.

Altekar, A.S., *Education in Ancient India*, Nand Kishore and Bros, Benaras, 1944.

Avinashlingam, T.S. (Ed.) *Education*, Compiled from speeches and writings of Vivekananda, Madras, 1957.

Bhattacharya, Hardas (Ed.), *The Cultural Heritage of India*, 4. Vols., The Ramakrishna Mission Institute of Culture, Calcutta, 1975.

Deway, John, *Democracy in Education*, MacMillan Co, New York, 1916.

Gupta, N.L., *Educational Ideals and Institutions in Mahabharata*, Mohit Publications, New Delhi 1998.

—, —, *Huministic Tradition of India*, Mohit Publications, New Delhi, 1999.

—, —, *Current Trends and Problems of Progressive Education*, Krishna Bros, Ajmer, 1985.

—,—, *Encyclopaedic Survey of Oriental Thought*, Vol.III, Anmol Publications Pvt. Ltd., New Delhi, 1999.

Kabir, Humayun, *Indian Philosophy of Education*, Asia Publishing House, 1951.

Romain Rolland, *Lift of Vivekananda and Universal Gospel*, translated by Malcolm Smith, Advati Ashram Calcutta, X impression, 1984.

Rao, V.K.R.N., *Swami Vivekananda.*

Swami Nirvedanand, *Swami Vivekananda on India and Her Problems*, Almora, 1971.

Sister Nivedita, *The Master as I Saw Him*, An intimate Study of Swami Vivekananda, education, 1939.

Whitehead, A.N., *Aims of Education and Other Essays*, Williams and Norgate, London, 1960.

Index

N

P

R

S

T

U

❑❑❑